Airport Demand Forecasting for Long-Term Planning

Roundtable Report

Please cite this publication as:
OECD (2016), *Airport Demand Forecasting for Long-Term Planning*, ITF Round Tables, OECD Publishing, Paris.
http://dx.doi.org/10.1787/9789282108024-en

ISBN 978-92-82-10801-7 (print)
ISBN 978-92-82-10802-4 (PDF)

Series: ITF Round Tables
ISSN 2074-3378 (print)
ISSN 2074-336X (online)

Photo credits: Cover © G. Tipene/shutterstock.com.

Corrigenda to OECD publications may be found on line at: *www.oecd.org/about/publishing/corrigenda.htm*.

The International Transport Forum

The International Transport Forum is an intergovernmental organisation with 57 member countries. It acts as a think tank for transport policy and organises the Annual Summit of transport ministers. ITF is the only global body that covers all transport modes. The ITF is politically autonomous and administratively integrated with the OECD.

The ITF works for transport policies that improve peoples' lives. Our mission is to foster a deeper understanding of the role of transport in economic growth, environmental sustainability and social inclusion and to raise the public profile of transport policy.

The ITF organises global dialogue for better transport. We act as a platform for discussion and pre-negotiation of policy issues across all transport modes. We analyse trends, share knowledge and promote exchange among transport decision-makers and civil society. The ITF's Annual Summit is the world's largest gathering of transport ministers and the leading global platform for dialogue on transport policy.

The Members of the ITF are: Albania, Armenia, Argentina, Australia, Austria, Azerbaijan, Belarus, Belgium, Bosnia and Herzegovina, Bulgaria, Canada, Chile, China (People's Republic of), Croatia, Czech Republic, Denmark, Estonia, Finland, France, Former Yugoslav Republic of Macedonia, Georgia, Germany, Greece, Hungary, Iceland, India, Ireland, Israel, Italy, Japan, Korea, Latvia, Liechtenstein, Lithuania, Luxembourg, Malta, Mexico, Republic of Moldova, Montenegro, Morocco, the Netherlands, New Zealand, Norway, Poland, Portugal, Romania, Russian Federation, Serbia, Slovak Republic, Slovenia, Spain, Sweden, Switzerland, Turkey, Ukraine, the United Kingdom and the United States.

International Transport Forum
2, rue André Pascal
F-75775 Paris Cedex 16
contact@itf-oecd.org
www.itf-oecd.org

ITF Roundtable Reports

ITF Roundtable Reports present the proceedings of ITF roundtable meetings, dedicated to specific topics notably on economic and regulatory aspects of transport policies in ITF member countries. Roundtable Reports contain the reviewed versions of the discussion papers presented by international experts at the meeting and a summary of discussions with the main findings of the roundtable. This work is published under the responsibility of the Secretary-General of the OECD. The opinions expressed and arguments employed herein do not necessarily reflect the official views of International Transport Forum member countries. This document and any map included herein are without prejudice to the status of or sovereignty over any territory, to the delimitation of international frontiers and boundaries and to the name of any territory, city or area

Table of contents

Tables

Figures

Executive summary

Decisions on expanding airport capacity are often controversial. Good transport infrastructure is of key importance for productivity and economic growth but airport capacity that is highly accessible to central city areas means that residents suffer more noise, air pollution and landscape degradation. In addition, airport assets are often long-lived with long lead times. Forecasts of future demand are thus a key tool for the consideration of extra capacity as well as to measure the economic benefits and costs of this extra capacity.

Air passenger markets are highly dynamic and strongly influenced by the regulatory environment. Markets that have been de-regulated have seen rapid growth as prices fell and new, low-cost business models emerged. Liberalisation also stimulated re-organisation of network services with concentration of demand on a few hub airports. Demand for air services increases rapidly as incomes rise, but the market is not homogenous and understanding the drivers of each market is critical. Long-term airport planning has to account for the risks entailed by these dynamics.

This report reviews the state of the art in forecasting airport demand. It focuses particularly on addressing demand risk, passenger behaviour and uncertainty and discusses how to make more effective use of such analysis in planning decisions.

Improving methodologies for air transport demand forecasting

Demand forecasts for the medium to long term are judged to be essential to the successful planning and delivery of major airport infrastructure. A recent review of airport demand forecasts in the United States concluded that econometric modelling has been an effective tool for generating medium to long-term forecasts of airport activity (ACRP, 2007). However, the track record of airport demand forecasting appears to be mixed, with illustrations of successes, but also failures in terms of a large divergence between forecast and out-turn. The first priority area is therefore to improve forecasts of airport demand. The report puts forward four key recommendations:

- **Use quantitative methods to analyse the key drivers of airport demand**

Econometric and statistical analysis can help in understanding the key drivers of past growth trends and help to build forecasts of how the level of airport demand might develop in the future. Two kinds of quantitative methods are discussed in detail:

- An approach based on the observed choices made by individual travellers (or groups), as between different possible destinations, modes, routes and airports and which uses this analysis as a basis for forecasting the likely development of future choices. Mandel (2014) presents a very comprehensive example of such an approach. That is, the econometric system approach developed by MKmetric to perform short and long-term air transport demand forecasts while considering various determinants such as socio-economy, policy, infrastructure and land use.

- An alternative, non-econometric approach of behaviour modelling is the 'Kenza' approach which was initially developed for Airbus Industrie by Sallier (2010) and represents, today, the primary short, medium and (very) long-term demand forecasting tool of Aéroports de Paris.

- **Use expert guidance to help interpret the quantitative results**

  Expert assessment, perhaps formalised through techniques such as Delphi, can help to understand where and why the models' analysis of the past might not fit the future and, in this way, to suggest appropriate modifications to the models' forecasting results.

- **Quality-assure the analysis and counter the risks of optimism bias**

  Quality assurance can help to improve the accuracy of forecasts and, equally important, assure stakeholders that the forecasts are unbiased, constraining the risks of optimism bias.

- **Reflect the risks and uncertainties that arise in even the best forecasts**

  Recognising risks and uncertainties can help to develop better investment strategies, which aim to control adverse risks and to reduce their negative impact in order to improve the overall efficiency and added value of infrastructure investment. An important example that is discussed in detail is the risk that the dynamics in airline network developments pose to airports. Scenario analysis can be effective approach to explore and exemplify the impact of these risks if it is conducted properly and with expert guidance.

Make better use of demand forecasts in airport infrastructure planning

The second priority area is to make better use of demand forecasts in airport infrastructure planning. InterVISTAS (2014) examined how risk and uncertainty can be addressed in airport traffic forecasting and airport planning. The research developed a unified systems analysis framework that enables airport activity forecasters to identify risk factors, to understand the extent to which each risk factor introduces uncertainty into activity forecasts, and to ascertain how the risks and uncertainties are likely to interact so as to examine realistically their combined implications for air traffic going forward.

The main purpose of recognising and quantifying risks and uncertainties in future airport demand is to help to develop useful risk management measures. Approaches divide into two broad groups:

- **Involve risk sharing**

  The aim here is to facilitate the control and/or diversification of risk, in particular, through vertical integration. Examples include:

  - Long-term contracts (between airline(s) and airport), which have been used to manage some of the demand side risks to the development of major infrastructure by providing some control over the risks of asset stranding, at airports in a competitive market setting.
  - Probabilistic forecasts which have been employed at Aéroports de Paris since 2003 for determining optimal points for new capacity, in terms of revenues and cost. This provides the information required for informed negotiation with airlines that request increased capacity. When demand appears insufficient from the airport's point of view airlines can be asked to pay a risk premium if they want the airport to build early.
  - Co-financing airport development.

- **Flexible strategic/dynamic strategic/adaptive planning**

  The aim of a flexible approach to infrastructure investment is to reduce the costs of unexpected traffic outcomes. Examples include:

- measures which make provision for future development without, at this stage, making a commitment to expand
- measures which make provision for incremental development as traffic levels develop
- measures which make provision for switching facilities between different types of traffic
- measures which make provision for different types of aircraft
- measures which retain flexibility in the start and/or completion dates for a project.

Finally, it is important to recognise that however successfully all of the foregoing is carried out, there are likely to remain material risks and uncertainties in even the best airport demand forecasts. The challenge is thus to make the residual uncertainty apparent to decision-makers without undermining the value attached to the economic appraisal of prospective investments.

In addition, it can be concluded that there is relatively limited rigorous evidence available on the ex post performance of airport demand forecasts. This should be a priority for future research.

Chapter 1. Summary of discussions

David Thompson[1],
Stephen Perkins[2] and Wouter de Wit[3]

Demand forecasts for the medium to long term are essential to the successful planning and delivery of major airport infrastructure but the track record of airport demand forecasting appears to be mixed. The first priority area is therefore to improve forecasts and the report puts forward four key recommendations:

- Use quantitative methods to analyse the key drivers of airport demand.

- Use expert guidance to help interpret the quantitative results.

- Quality-assure the analysis and counter the risks of optimism bias.

- Reflect the risks and uncertainties that arise in even the best forecasts.

The second priority is to make effective use of demand forecasts in airport infrastructure planning. The main purpose of recognising and quantifying risks and uncertainties in future airport demand is to help to develop useful risk management measures. Approaches divide into two broad groups:

- Risk sharing arrangements.

- Flexible strategic/dynamic strategic/adaptive planning.

Thirdly, it is important to recognize that however successfully all of the foregoing is carried out, there are likely to remain material risks and uncertainties in even the best airport demand forecasts. The challenge is thus to make the residual uncertainty apparent to decision-makers without undermining the value attached to the economic appraisal of prospective investments.

1. Independent consultant.

2. International Transport Forum

3. International Transport Forum

Introduction

Expanding airport capacity in cities is both important and controversial. It is characterised by a fundamental trade-off between economic and environmental goals. Good transport infrastructure is of key importance for productivity and economic growth but airport capacity that is highly accessible to central city areas means that residents suffer more noise, air pollution and landscape degradation (in addition to the wider impacts of additional greenhouse emissions). Experience around the world shows that this trade-off is an important and contentious policy issue, and that there are no straightforward solutions (ITF, 2014)) for an overview of these issues.

Demand forecasts are an essential tool for the consideration of extra capacity. Growth in air travel signals the importance of connectivity, but also drives increasing pressure on capacity. Airport assets are often, but not always, long-lived with long lead times. Forecasts of future demand are thus a key determinant of the case for adding capacity. And forecasting tools are also needed to measure the economic benefits and costs of this extra capacity.

Research to underpin forecasts has been extensive but large uncertainties remain. Understanding fully the drivers of past growth helps, including the impacts of past regulatory reform, longer term macro-economic and demographic trends, and innovation in technologies and business models. Understanding the likely future path of these key long term drivers, following the great recession, is important. Understanding if and when the strong historic link between growth in incomes and in air travel demand might start to weaken is important in the more mature markets. Understanding the effects of future innovations in supply (including high-speed rail in short haul markets) is critical and often particularly difficult.

Forecasts are also prone to well-recognised risks of quality shortfall or of institutional biases. Quality issues may arise when forecasts fail to reflect current best practice (proportionate to the task in hand) and there is always a risk of optimism bias to forecasts. And this, in turn, can make credibility an issue with stakeholders.

These risks, together with the uncertainties of unforeseen events – the "unknown unknowns" - mean that airport demand forecasts are a difficult challenge. Understanding the past is not easy and, and as Nils Bohr famously remarked, "prediction is very difficult, especially if it's about the future".

Overview of emerging findings

Airport demand forecasts are both difficult and very important. The discussions at the Roundtable suggested a paradox:

- On the one hand, it was recognised that airport demand forecasts are often problematic – with a track record which shows some major surprises, in terms of a large divergence between forecast and out-turn.
- On the other hand, demand forecasts for the medium to long term were judged to be essential to the successful planning and delivery of major airport infrastructure.

The Roundtable papers and discussions highlighted a wide breadth of research evidence and expertise which together can help in making progress on this fundamental dilemma. Progress is required on two fronts.

The first priority area is to improve forecasts of airport demand. The track record of airport demand forecasting appears to be mixed – with illustrations of both successes and failures. Nevertheless, a recent review of airport demand forecasts in the United States concluded that econometric modelling has been an effective tool for generating medium to long term forecasts of airport activity (whilst recognizing the potential pitfalls and noting the need for more research on how well forecasts have performed in practice), ACRP (2007). The Roundtable reached similar conclusions, and discussed various steps that might help to improve airport demand forecasts.

The second priority area is to make better use of demand forecasts in airport infrastructure planning. The aim here is to recognise the risks and uncertainties that will arise in even the best airport demand forecasts. And then, secondly, to use this analysis to help develop investment strategies that aim either to control adverse risks (that is, reduce the chances of their happening) and/or reduce their negative impacts (in the event that these adverse risks do happen in practice). And so, in this way, improve the efficiency and value of airport infrastructure investment. This is the subject of the final section of the paper.

Making better forecasts of airport demand

An overarching theme of the emerging findings on demand forecasts is the value to be gained from blending together quantitative analysis - based on econometric and statistical methods - and qualitative analysis, drawing upon expert assessment.

First, it will usually be worthwhile to use econometric and statistical analysis, of the kind elaborated in the Roundtable papers, to help understand – in quantitative terms – the key drivers that have shaped demand in the past; and use this as a starting point to forecast future demand. Consideration will need to be given to the relative merits of time series analysis or choice analysis - where the former has strengths in relation to understanding the long term socio-economic drivers of demand and the latter is particularly useful where passengers' choices – between mode, airline or airport – are a strong driver of demand. Decisions on the best forecasting method to adopt should be shaped by an assessment of prospective market circumstances. But sometimes, perhaps often, a two-stage approach will provide the best solution – using time-series econometrics to develop forecasts for a broadly defined market and choice analysis to develop forecasts for specific airports within this market, especially when airports compete for overlapping markets.

Second, it will be useful to draw upon expert guidance, perhaps using formal elicitation methods (such as Delphi exercises) to make best use of this expertise. Expert guidance will be particularly helpful in the choice of forecasting methods (as discussed above) and in advising on the interpretation of the emerging results and the development of forecasts from these results – in particular, assessing how far the past is likely to provide a good guide to the future and, if not, in what ways model parameters should be amended to reflect this. And expert guidance will also be valuable in building scenarios – that is, alternative future paths of development – for those key demand drivers that cannot be predicted with any useful precision. Scenario analysis is likely to be particularly helpful in considering the future development of airline networks, and the associated implications of this for competition and service provision at different airports.

Third, it will be important to constrain the risks of optimism bias. Here expert guidance on emerging forecasts – as described above – and independent peer review will be helpful, together with transparency and engagement with the broad range of stakeholders with an interest in the forecasts, and through the benchmarking of forecasts to the existing research literature. For example, Gillen, Morrison and Stewart (2002) provide a summary of research evidence on price and income elasticity. InterVISTAS (2007) also provides an overview and suggests some comparators, as does Oum, Fu and Zhang (2009).

Finally, we need to recognise that however successfully all of the foregoing is carried out, there are likely to remain material risks and uncertainties in even the best airport demand forecasts. The key issues this raises are twofold. First, there is the question of how risks and uncertainties should best be measured, and in this way recognised, in the presentation of airport demand forecasts. That is, how we can be (appropriately) more modest in presenting forecasts. The second question is how these risks and uncertainties are best taken into consideration in the planning of airport infrastructure investment, with the aim of controlling adverse risks and/or reducing their negative impact, and in this way improving the efficiency and value of infrastructure investment. The challenge is thus to make the residual uncertainty apparent to decision-makers without undermining the value attached to the economic appraisal of prospective investments.

Making better use of demand forecasts

Consideration of how best to reflect risk and uncertainty suggests a second important paradox. On the one hand, risk and uncertainty are acknowledged to be an important characteristic of airport demand forecasts, with important consequences. On the other hand, these risks and uncertainties are often not subject to serious analytical consideration, nor are they recognised, in an effective way, in investment planning. The Roundtable papers and discussions suggest that tools are being developed to do both.

As far as analysing risks and uncertainties is concerned, there will again be advantages to an approach which blends together the quantitative and the qualitative. That is, an approach which first uses techniques such as Monte Carlo analysis to get quantitative measures of the risks and uncertainties which are "in the model", using econometric and statistical analysis of past data. But an approach which also recognises that a model that successfully fits the past may not equally fit the future, and which uses expert opinion – perhaps codified using formal elicitation techniques – to consider whether and how additional risks should be added to the model's forecasts. In some cases, there will be a sufficient research base to develop useful subjective probabilities to supplement, or substitute, those suggested by the model. In other cases where uncertainties are greater, then expert opinion can help develop plausible alternative scenarios, even if it is not possible to sensibly say which, if any, of these scenarios is most likely to happen in practice. The value of such scenarios is both to reveal the scale of uncertainty and to provide a basis for testing the robustness of a project to uncertainty.

A particularly important source of uncertainty discussed at the Roundtable, where scenario analysis is likely to be worthwhile, relates to future airline network development. Whilst the research evidence shows that levels of air service are often an important factor in shaping passengers' choices – and hence airport demand - the airline business decisions which determine service levels are less well researched and the findings are less clear cut.

In summary, most theoretical studies of airline networks suggest that it is usually beneficial – in economic and commercial terms – for a network airline to focus its operations in a particular market on a single hub, although some studies nevertheless suggest that a multi-hub network may sometimes prove more efficient – perhaps in situations where there is strong geographic segmentation between different parts of the market, together with sufficient local O-D demand. And it is also possible that at very high levels of traffic there might be various diseconomies of hub size which start to off-set the benefits of density economies.

Recent empirical research in the USA (ACRP, 2013) provides some support for these findings. In particular, the study found that airlines prefer to concentrate services in a particular region at as few airports as possible, although larger carriers will sometimes operate at more than one airport in a large metropolitan region if the demand conditions provide for this. More generally, the provision of airline services at secondary airports is usually found to be shaped by the suitability of these airports for the provision of niche services by low cost carriers. These carriers tend to focus on point to point traffic, and this means that they usually choose to serve a region through a single gateway.

Experience in Europe also supports these emerging conclusions showing, first, a number of unsuccessful attempts to establish dual or split hubs (in particular, Rome-Milan Malpensa, Heathrow-Gatwick and Madrid-Barcelona). This lack of success seems to reflect the economic advantages of a single hub; and in the case of Milan, also strong competition from a well-established and highly accessible short-haul airport at Milan Linate. However, the European experience also shows, secondly, a number of examples of legacy hubs – that is hubs inherited from the regulated era – which have been successfully sustained in a multi-hub network (for example, Paris-Amsterdam, London-Madrid or Lufhthansa's configuration, constructed around its primary hub at Frankfurt). The continuing success of these multiple hubs seems in many cases to reflect a degree of complementarity, with relatively strong geographic segmentation in their markets, typically the various partner hubs are located in different European countries with different historic patterns of trade and business connections – Burghouwt (2013), perhaps also reinforced by passengers' general preferences to continue using a familiar airport. However, in some other cases – for example Lufthansa's secondary and tertiary hubs at Munich and Dusseldorf – their role appears to be primarily about offering additional direct services to supplement those from the primary hub at Frankfurt, in part reflecting the evolution of capacity constraints there (see Burghouwt (2013) for a discussion of "overflow" hubs).

Finally, these uncertainties on the path of airline network development are likely to compound as we look into the future, as developments in technology bring further changes. In particular, the introduction of smaller, lower cost aircraft (such as the Airbus A350 or the Boeing Dreamliner) on long-haul services, coupled with rising demand levels as the world economy starts to recover from the Great Recession, are likely to bring a greater role for point to point services, quite possibly provided from non-hub airports, although these types of aircraft will also support the provision of additional thinner routes from existing hubs.

More generally, in presenting measures of risk and uncertainty it will be important to be transparent about which risks are included in the quantitative analysis (and which are not) and about the methods used to estimate these. It will also be important to be similarly clear about the use of subjective probabilities (and the provenance for these) and the evidence underpinning the scenario development used to consider the uncertainties, which cannot be included in the quantitative risk analysis.

The main purpose of recognising and quantifying (where possible) risks and uncertainties is to help to develop useful risk management measures. Thus the aim is not simply to predict how risky and uncertain a proposed investment project might be. Rather the aim is to help develop investment strategies which either help to control adverse risks (by reducing the chances of their happening) and/or which help to reduce their negative impact upon financial and economic returns (in circumstances where the risk nevertheless does happen; and, of course, vice versa for upside risks). The overall goal here is to help, in this way, to improve the overall efficiency and added value of infrastructure investment.

The emerging evidence discussed at the Roundtable suggested productive ways of achieving this, and thus making airport infrastructure investment more robust to the risks and uncertainties in future airport demand. Approaches divide into two sometimes complementary groups:

- The first involves risk sharing; the aim here is to facilitate control of an adverse risk (that is, to reduce the chances of it happening in practice) and/or to diversify some of the consequences – in particular, through vertical integration.
- The second approach involves a flexible approach to infrastructure investment – sometimes called flexible strategic planning; the aim here is to reduce the (net) costs that would arise if the adverse risk does happen in practice (and vice versa for upside risks, of course).

As the discussion in the previous section illustrates, an important risk to the demand forecasts for some airports – those which face a material degree of competition – is the possibility that key customer airlines may choose to relocate their business to a competitor airport. This carries the risk of under-utilised and under-remunerated infrastructure – and this risk may in turn weaken investment incentives. A common business solution to these sorts of problem is some form of vertical integration, with the aim of assigning particular risks to the parties best able to control the risk and/or to diversify it. See, for example, Kay (1993) for an overview. In the case of airports, the regulatory reforms of the last several decades have both prompted and facilitated widespread innovation in organisation and ownership (see

Gillen (2011) for a review). And these developing business arrangements quite often involve vertical relationships between airports and airlines. In practice, vertical relationships take a range of forms. For example, David Starkie (2012) discusses the role of long term contracts between airline(s) and airport that have been used to manage some of the demand-side risks to the development of major infrastructure at airports in a competitive market setting, by providing some control over the risks of asset stranding. Another example is provided by the various different methods which are sometimes used to, in effect, co-finance airport development (Fu, Homsobat and Oum, 2011). And a further example discussed at the Roundtable is provided by Paris where probabilistic forecasts have been employed since 2003 (Sallier 2010). Optimal points for new capacity, in terms of revenues and costs are determined. This provides the information required for informed negotiation with airlines that request increased capacity. When demand appears insufficient from the airport's point of view airlines can be asked to pay a risk premium if they want the airport to build early. This kind of risk premium can probably be hedged on financial markets.

It is important to recognise that the benefits of vertical links may run wider than just the facilitation of investment in long term infrastructure at airports in a competitive market setting. For example, vertical links may also be important to sustaining service quality in the face of unexpected adverse shocks (e.g. shocks related to weather or to security threats), where trust and co-operation between different parts of the supply chain will often be important to sustaining service quality.

Of course, it also needs to be recognised that long term vertical relationships carry the risk of anti-competitive restriction, where a vertical link might be used to raise the costs of market entry. There is therefore likely to be a balance of both benefits and costs to at least some vertical links. Competition authorities will need to be alert to this trade off, and the balance of benefits and costs will need to be assessed on a case by case basis. This will not be straightforward. However, the risks of an anti-competitive restraint will generally be greatest in circumstances where an airport has material market power; and this is also where the risks of expropriation/asset stranding are also likely to be least strong (and vice versa).Transparency of vertical links will also be important (although not necessarily straightforward to achieve).

It also needs to be recognised that vertical relationships can only improve the control of risks which are endogenous to the aviation business (for example, the risk that an airline will choose to move more of its business to an alternative airport). Vertical integration won't improve the control of exogenous risks (for example, a downturn in the economy), although it might help with the diversification of such risks.

Whilst risk sharing can thus help to control, or to diversify, the risks associated with airport demand forecasts, the aim of taking a flexible approach to infrastructure investment is to reduce the net costs of downside risks being realised in practice (or to increase the net benefit, in the case of favourable surprises).The basic idea behind this approach is to retain flexibility, either in the scale of the infrastructure – by holding open the possibility of adding to (or subtracting from) the intended capacity – and/or in the timing of the proposed investment, holding open the possibility of deferring or advancing the investment. The aim of retaining flexibility in these ways is to help respond quickly to unexpected traffic outcomes and, in this way, to achieve a better fit between the volume of capacity which is provided and that which turns out to be actually needed in practice. The approach is sometimes described in a real options framework. That is, an infrastructure project is developed in a way which holds open a series of options (essentially to do more or less) which can be taken up in response to changing circumstances (or not, if the central forecasts turn out to be realised).

Of course, flexibility of this type will usually come at a price. That is, holding open an option will usually add to costs. And it will usually, therefore, be less good value to do this in circumstances where demand is broadly in line with the central airport demand forecast. The key question is then how much value is added by a flexible solution in circumstances where there are unexpected traffic outcomes; and whether these unexpected outcomes are sufficiently likely to occur in practice, such as to make the flexible option a good investment.

The discussions at the Roundtable suggested that a flexible approach can sometimes (and perhaps often) be worthwhile. Flexible solutions include, in particular:

- measures that make provision for future development without, at this stage, making a commitment to expand
- measures that make provision for incremental development as traffic levels develop
- measures that make provision for switching facilities between different types of traffic (e.g. international and domestic), for example, through flexible gates
- measures that make provision for different types of aircraft
- measures that retain flexibility in the start and/or completion dates for a project.

Whilst there is a wide menu of flexible solutions which have been found to work in practice, in order to be successful they will usually need to be tailored to the specific market circumstances (current and prospective) of the airport under consideration. The Roundtable paper by Ian Kincaid and Nicole Geitebruegge of InterVISTAS (Kincaid and Geitebruegge 2014) notes that "there is no standalone method or tool that can offer the correct set of strategies" and suggests an approach which builds upon current practice (where ACRP (2012) offers a series of case studies) and then uses expert advice from airport stakeholders and subject experts to suggest solutions which are feasible and relevant to the particular airport under consideration.

The evaluation of whether particular flexible solutions are worthwhile can involve qualitative appraisal, based on expert judgement, and this is sometimes sufficient to provide a clear conclusion. In other cases a quantitative appraisal – which aims to measure the expected cost benefit return – will provide a more robust basis for decisions; although of course to do this requires some reasonable estimates of the probabilities of different scenarios for traffic growth (for example, using results from the kinds of Monte Carlo analysis described earlier; more details are provided in the Roundtable paper by Kincaid and Geitebruegge).

Several case studies of the practical implementation of flexible infrastructure solutions in North America are documented in the ACRP report mentioned earlier (see ACRP (2012), whilst Burghouwt (2007) provides a detailed case study of flexible investment planning at Amsterdam airport. Although many of the examples of flexible infrastructure work at a relatively micro level – expansion of (a part of) an individual terminal, for example – the principles of flexible strategic planning can equally be usefully applied on a larger scale. For example, de Neufville (1995) considers a choice between the development of Amsterdam airport versus the possibility of a new offshore airport; he judges this latter possibility to be an unwise commitment in a flexible planning framework. More generally still, the UK Airports Commission are following an approach that might be characterised as an application of flexible strategic planning at the level of the whole London airports market.

Drawing all this together, elements of a good projection exercise with the right blend of quantitative analysis and qualitative expert assessment are as follows.

- **Use quantitative methods to analyse the key drivers of airport demand.**

  Econometric and statistical analysis can help in understanding the key drivers of past growth trends and, in this way, help to build forecasts of how the level of airport demand might develop in the future.

- **Use expert guidance to help interpret the quantitative results.**

  Expert assessment – perhaps formalised through techniques such as Delphi – can help to understand where and why the models' analysis of the past might not fit the future and, in this way, to suggest appropriate modifications to the models' forecasting results.

- **Reflect the risks and uncertainties that arise in even the best forecasts.**

  Recognising risks and uncertainties can help to develop better investment strategies which aim to control adverse risks, and/or to reduce their negative impact, and in this way can help to improve the overall efficiency and added value of infrastructure investment. Reflecting risks and uncertainties in the forecasts can involve:

  - Using analytical methods (such as Monte Carlo) to measure risks which can be quantified (that is, risks which are "in the model" such as uncertainties on demand elasticity).
  - Using scenario analysis to explore and exemplify the impact of risks which can be recognised, but whose likelihood cannot be realistically estimated (for example, the shape of future airline network development).
  - Using event analysis to illustrate the possible impact of "unknown-unknowns".

- **Quality-assure the analysis and counter the risks of optimism bias.**

  Quality assurance can help to improve the accuracy of forecasts and, equally important, assure stakeholders that the forecasts are unbiased. Quality assurance can involve:

  - expert peer review of methods, results and forecasts – using collaborative "critical friends"
  - benchmarking of results against the research literature
  - transparency through the publication of methods and results, and engagement with stakeholders through discussion forums.

- **Deploy resource efforts proportional to the task in hand.**

  For large, irreversible, risky investments it is worth investing in the highest quality of forecasting analysis which is available, and getting the best possible understanding of risks and uncertainties. At the other end of the scale – for smaller, reversible, less risky investments – then less investment in analysis is likely to be worthwhile and in some cases market testing ("suck it and see") may be the best way forward.

Improving forecasts of airport demand

The basic problem identified with airport demand forecasts in the Roundtable discussions is a track record which sometimes shows major surprises – in terms of a big divergence between forecast and out-turn. The Roundtable papers provide some illustrations of this (Figure 2.1 from the Roundtable paper by Ian Kincaid and Nicole Geitebruegge), although, of course, some forecasts have proved to be more successful (ACRP (2012) for a range of case studies).

Hyderabad's new airport provides a further example. Forecasts before the airport was built proved completely wrong. Domestic deregulation caused an unforeseen explosion of traffic whilst international traffic didn't grow as expected because of bilateral constraints, and whilst the airport was intended to become a hub, no hub developed as no locally based airline emerged to operate one. It must always be remembered that hubs are built by airlines not airports. As Brian Pearce noted in his presentation to the meeting "forecasts fail - just when you need them".

As discussed in the introduction, all of this matters because investment in airport infrastructure is often lumpy and irreversible (with long lead times) and is often politically controversial. This in turn means that forecasts which provide a poor prediction of out-turn carry the risk of potentially costly mistakes in infrastructure planning, in terms either of the scale and/or the timing of investment. Furthermore, a poor forecasting track record will often act to weaken support for investments which are politically contentious, because the underlying demand forecasts appear open to reasonable disagreement. For both these reasons (identifying infrastructure investments that are worthwhile and then sustaining political and public support for such investment) it is important to develop forecasts that command both confidence and support (as well as recognizing the risks and uncertainties which will arise in even the best forecasts and developing investment strategies which aim to control adverse risks and reduce their negative impact).

Two further points are worth noting by way of introduction. The first is that whilst the track record of airport demand forecasting appears to be mixed – with some illustrations of both successes and failures as noted above – in practice there is very limited rigorous analytical evidence with which to form a judgement on the overall success of airport demand forecasting and the relative merits of different approaches. A recent report on airport demand forecasts in the USA identified this gap in our knowledge as a priority for future research (ACRP (2007) and the Roundtable discussions reached some similar conclusions.

Secondly, it is worth emphasizing that in the context of infrastructure development – which was the frame of reference for the Roundtable – then what is of most relevance are demand forecasts for the medium to long term. Short term shocks are of course immensely important for shaping near term operating decisions and for near term profitability. Equally they are also often very difficult to forecast, for example, the particular impact upon air services of volcanic activity. But unless short term shocks impact (materially) upon longer term demand, then the implications for infrastructure development are less significant. What matters in this context is the robustness of longer term forecasts of airport demand, which in the context of infrastructure development will need to encompass various airport activities including, in particular, passenger numbers and aircraft movements together with an analysis of prospective peaking patterns.

The Roundtable discussions showed that there is a wealth of high quality research evidence – and high quality expertise – upon which to draw in preparing medium/long term forecasts of airport demand. The discussion at the Roundtable suggested that making the best use of this expertise needed to involve both:

- choosing the right forecasting approaches ,and
- getting the best out of the models used.

We will consider each of these in turn.

Choosing the forecasting approach

A number of forecasting approaches exist, embracing both qualitative and quantitative methods (ACRP, 2007 and IATA, 2008). A degree of modesty is advisable with any approach and the object of modelling should be to illustrate and make evident the important factors and the major risks involved in shaping demand rather than to pretend that it is possible to produce an accurate picture of any specific moment in the future. Models take a variety of forms ranging from Delphi surveys to discrete choice modelling. This section briefly outlines the most important models which are used in practice.

To start with, the Delphi study technique is a structured communication exercise aimed at producing detailed critical examination and discussion of issues. Developed in the 1950s and 1960s by the Rand Corporation, the technique was designed to elicit the opinions of experts in a particular field in a systematic way. It has been described as a "succession of iterative brainstorming rounds" and is suited to forecasting complex problems and it is a tool for gaining input from recognised sources of expertise. The Air Transport Research Society uses the Delphi study techniques at their annual conferences (Mason and Alamdari (2007). IATA has used similar methods although lately it relies more on 'average opinions' and consensus building than on Delphi studies, which according to the official definition of the technique requires, among other things, anonymous contributions from the experts (Mason and Alamdari (2007). More generally, Figure 2.4 from the Roundtable paper by Ian Kincaid and Nicole Geitebruegge provides an overview of the pros and cons of the main methods for eliciting and summarizing expert opinion.

Qualitative approaches thus provide a systematic route to tapping expert knowledge in ways that can yield valuable insights. And we will go on to argue below that this should be an essential part of airport demand forecasts. Nevertheless, qualitative approaches are subject to well-known weaknesses – in particular, the risks that the experts are over- confident in their assessments, and that there are halo effects (a tendency, for example, to favour particular businesses or individuals) and confirmation biases (interpreting new information as supporting prior beliefs). All of this suggests that whilst qualitative approaches are valuable, they may best be used in addition to (rather than instead of) more quantitative approaches.

On these latter, a recent survey of airport demand forecasts in the United States (ACRP, 2007) identifies three broad categories of quantitative forecasting methods:

- market-share forecasting
- time series modelling
- econometric modelling.

The first of these – market-share forecasting – is quite extensively used, but is relatively unsophisticated. In essence, this method assumes that demand at the particular airport under consideration will in the future take some pre-specified share of total air traffic in some broader market (for example, the relevant country or region). Using forecasts for air traffic in the broader market and assumptions on the relevant airport's market share of this (usually the present share, perhaps modified by judgmental adjustment to reflect anticipated market developments) yields a forecast for future air traffic at the airport under consideration. This method would be expected to break down if the relevant airport's market share changes in the future in an unexpected way. For this reason, the ACRP report (ACRP, 2007) does not recommend this approach to forecasting, whilst recognizing that it is often used in circumstances where there is inadequate data or where resources are not available to develop more sophisticated forecasts.

The second approach – time series modelling – essentially extrapolates past trends forwards into the future, without using independent explanatory variables. In other words, this approach doesn't include economic variables that attempt to explain how key drivers might have shaped past growth in airport demand; nor, in consequence, how they might shape future demand. For this reason, this approach is of limited value in assessing the impact upon demand of alternative infrastructure projects (or other policies) or of different scenarios for developments in the economy, consumer preferences or technologies. The ACRP report concludes, however, that time series analysis can be a useful approach for short term forecasts, particularly where there are complex time relationships relating to seasonality and trend.

The third approach – econometric modelling – is the most analytically sophisticated (and also the most demanding of data) and the ACRP report concluded that it was an effective tool for generating forecasts of airport activity. The Roundtable discussion reached a similar conclusion. The ACRP report notes a distinction between two different approaches to this type of analysis:

- An approach which uses time series econometrics to help understand the key drivers which have shaped past trends in demand and which then uses this analysis as a basis for forecasting the likely path of future demand. See ACRP (2007) for an overview of this approach and Airports Commission (2013) for an example of its application.
- An approach which is based on the observed choices made by individual travellers (or groups), as between different possible destinations, modes, routes and airports and which uses this analysis as a basis for forecasting the likely development of future choices (see the Roundtable paper by Benedikt Mandel for an overview; a recent ACRP report (ACRP (2013) also provides an overview and a survey of research literature.

The time series econometrics approach is well established in airport demand forecasting. This analysis can often provide a good understanding of the factors driving past trends (ACRP (2007) for a discussion). Nevertheless, it has sometimes proved difficult to confidently unpack the separate contributions of different drivers. For example, the discussion in Oum, Fu and Zhang (2009) suggests that the positive impacts upon demand of the regulatory reforms of the last several decades have sometimes been misattributed (at least partially) to the underlying trend growth in incomes and trade; the consequence is a risk of undue optimism about the impact which future growth in incomes and trade might have upon airport demand; in other words, an overestimate of the income elasticity. Combining time series and cross-sectional data (in a panel), where feasible, may help here (InterVISTAS (2007) for an illustration and a discussion of the challenges in robustly estimating income elasticity), and benchmarking against the research literature should also help (Gillen, Morrison and Stewart (2002) for a useful survey of research findings on price and income elasticity, and also InterVISTAS, 2007).

More generally, there is always a question of whether trends which have been well established in the past will hold equally true in the future. For example, whether the strong historic link which has been established between airport demand and economic growth will continue into the future, particularly as the centre of economic gravity moves eastwards with strong passenger demand growth in south-east Asia, or whether instead it will start to weaken, as suggested in the case of car travel (ITF/OECD (2013) for a discussion of this latter point, and Smyth and Christodoulou (2011) for a review of the rather limited research evidence on market maturity in air travel).

And finally, time series econometrics is usually a less useful forecasting tool in markets where there is the possibility of material changes in the degree of competition between airports and /or airlines. The regulatory reforms of recent decades, and collateral innovations in technologies and business models, have together meant that airlines and airports often face greater competition and, correspondingly, passengers have a wider range of alternatives to choose from. In consequence, these choices have become a far more important factor in shaping airport demand over this period (although the significance of this will of course vary between locations). It is in these circumstances that choice analysis is likely to be particularly useful (ACRP (2007), and it is to this that we now turn.

Choice analysis

An option that offers the possibility to examine potential outcomes in more detail is discrete choice modelling. This is used to analyse and predict individual choices between alternatives from a finite set of mutually exclusive and collectively exhaustive alternatives. Such models have numerous applications since many behavioural responses correspond to choices within a set of alternatives. The ultimate interest in discrete choice modelling, as in most modelling, lies in being able to predict the decision making behaviour of a group of users. The technique is used to determine the relative influence of different attributes of alternatives, and differing characteristics of individuals, when they make choices (Koppelman and Bhat, 2006).

There are two basic ways of modelling such group behaviour. The first is commonly referred to as the aggregate approach and directly models the aggregate share of all, or a segment of, users choosing each alternative as a function of the characteristics of the alternatives and socio-demographic attributes of the group. The second approach is to recognise that aggregate behaviour is the result of numerous individual decisions and to model individual choice responses as a function of the characteristics of the alternatives available to, and socio-demographic attributes of, each individual. This second approach is referred to as the disaggregate approach. While the second approach can provide much more information, it is also time-consuming and costly as it requires a lot of data, difficult to obtain in the airline industry (Koppelman and Bhat, 2006). One advantage of more aggregated models is that they tend to be more robust to the impact of short term perturbations and reflect long term trends. Highly disaggregate models can thus, paradoxically, be more prone to error than simpler models.

Discrete choice models are usually derived under an assumption of utility-maximizing behaviour by the decision maker. They describe preferences and choice in terms of probabilities of choosing each alternative rather than predicting that an individual will choose a particular mode with certainty. As with deterministic choice theory, the individual is assumed to choose an alternative if its utility is greater than that of any other alternative. As a result it can forecast what share of the population is likely to choose a certain alternative.

Logit, probit or linear probability models

The first two models fit curves to the data, incorporating saturation and gradual take-off effects at the upper and lower ends, in place of the straight line fits to the data points used in linear models. Logit regression models estimate the probability of choosing a certain alternative as a cumulative standard logistic distribution function, while probit regression does the same by using the cumulative normal probability distribution. Both methods provide very similar results, but historically logit models were easier to work with and as a result have been used the most (Koppelman and Bhat, 2006). When two alternatives are taken into account binary logistic models can be used. However, multinomial logit models (MNLs) should be used in the case of more than two alternatives. The MNL structure has been widely used for both urban and intercity mode choice models, primarily due to its simple mathematical form, ease of estimation and interpretation and the ability to add or remove choice alternatives. However, the MNL model has been widely criticised because of a property to treat as independent, irrelevant alternatives. This "IIA property" implies that for any individual, the probability of choosing an alternative is independent of the presence or attributes of any other alternative. The premise is that other alternatives are irrelevant to the decision of choosing between the two alternatives in the pair. This simplification does, however, allow the addition or removal of an alternative from the choice set without affecting the structure or parameters of the model. This leads to the flexibility of applying the model to cases with different choices, which has a number of advantages. First, the model can be estimated and applied in cases where different members of the population (and sample) face different sets of alternatives. Second, this property simplifies the estimation of the parameters in the multinomial logit model and third, this property is advantageous when applying a model to the prediction of choice probabilities for a new alternative (Koppelman and Bhat, 2006).

On the other hand, the IIA property may not properly reflect the behavioural relationships among groups of alternatives as other alternatives may not be irrelevant to the ratio of probabilities between a pair of alternatives. One of the most important restrictions of the IIA property implies that introduction of a new mode, or improvements to any existing mode, will reduce the attraction of existing modes in proportion to their probability of being chosen before the change. This is likely to lead to misleading results in cases where some alternatives are more 'similar' than others.

A simple example is mode choice among automobile, bus transit, and rail transit, as described in Small and Verhoef (2007). The two public transit modes have many unmeasured attributes in common, such as occasional crowding. Suppose a traveller initially has available only auto and bus, with equal systematic utilities so that the choice probabilities are each one-half. Now suppose we want to predict the effects of adding a rail service with measurable characteristics identical to those for bus. The MNL models would predict that all three modes would then have choice probabilities of one-third; in reality, the probability of choosing auto would most likely remain near one-half while the two transit modes divide the rest of the probability equally between them. The argument is even stronger if we imagine instead that the newly added mode is simply a bus of a different colour: this is the famous "red bus, blue bus" example of Small and Verhoef.

A nested logit model can provide a solution here as it corrects for this by using a nested (tree) structure that allows for correlation for a subset (i.e. nest) of alternatives. As a result complex tree structures can be developed which offer substantial flexibility in representing differential 'competitiveness' between pairs of alternatives. A disadvantage is that the nesting structure imposes a system of restrictions concerning relationships between pairs of alternatives (Koppelman and Bhat, 2006).

An alternative and very different type of behaviour modelling is the"Kenza" approach developed by Sallier (2010). He came up with an empirical, non-econometric approach in an attempt to overcome some of the perceived disadvantages of econometric projection. Econometric forecasts require a reasonable length of times series data to provide a projection with reasonable suppression of noise in the data (or, perhaps, a panel of time series and cross-sectional data). Such long time series data are sometimes not available, or of limited use because of the impact of 'exceptional' events occurring during the period recorded. Secondly, any econometric model extrapolates over the future the pattern of (consumer) behaviour measured in the past. This can be considered a rather questionable assumption as future behaviour patterns may change.

Sallier therefore uses a more behavioural modelling approach in order to assess how demand elasticities might evolve in the future. His demand equation uses average ticket prices, normalised in relation to incomes (normalization value), while reflecting customer behaviour via the use of parameters operating on ticket prices (reservation price) and market penetration rates (rate of entry). Sallier assumes the parameters to be constant over time, but different from one population to another, and assumes that individuals tend to adopt the qualitative and quantitative consuming habits typical of current air travellers as soon as their income increases to levels that allow them to do so. This is a strong assumption that may not hold in reality. However, this simplification does allow Sallier to use a relatively simple and static model which he considers does not have to deal with endogeneity and time series problems typical of econometric analysis. The Kenza approach was initially developed for Airbus Industries in the late 90s and represents, today, the primary short, medium and (very) long term demand forecasting tool of Aéroports de Paris (CDG & Orly).

More generally, a developing research literature is improving our understanding of the factors which are important to shaping passenger choices between different airports (see, for example, ACRP (2013) and the Roundtable presentation by Benedikt Mandel, which outlines a model in which passengers choose between different origin and destination airports – within a regional catchment – and between competing route alternatives). The emerging evidence reviewed in the ACRP report confirms that, as expected, two of the most important factors are an airport's effective catchment area – its accessibility to prospective passengers – and various characteristics of the level of air service offered (particularly frequency of flights).

The impact of these factors differs, as expected, between passenger segments (for example, leisure travellers are usually more willing to travel to a distant airport, but usually put less value on a high flight frequency) and passengers usually tend to prefer airports with which they have (favourable) prior experience (referred to as "airport choice inertia" by Hess and Polak (2005) and related to Levine's concept of "familiarization" (Levine (1987), in which the search costs which passengers have sunk in a familiar airport/terminal/airline provide a competitive advantage to incumbents, which is sometimes reinforced through loyalty programmes).

Airline, ticket prices are an important airport choice factor for some (but not all) market segments, and there are several choice factors (e.g. length of check in time) which appear relevant to some specific locations, but not for all. The key question for airport demand is then how these different factors impact and interact in different locations and in different market settings (ACRP, 2013) for some illuminating case studies).

Whilst the level of air service is one of the most important factors shaping passengers' choice of airport, the ACRP report found that there is far less research evidence upon the factors which determine such levels of service at different airports (ACRP (2013). This is perhaps not surprising, given the profound changes which have taken place in the airline business over the last several decades – facilitated by wide ranging regulatory reform and stimulated by innovation in both business models and technologies. Anticipating the outcome of the development of increasingly competitive markets is, by their nature, very difficult. But what this means is that in using choice models to make forecasts we need to recognise that one of the key drivers of passengers' choices – levels of service - is itself very difficult to forecast. This suggests two conclusions. First, it means that this factor – the future pattern of development of airline services – will be a very important source of risk and uncertainty in the demand forecasts for at least some airports. The second conclusion is that there will be an important role for expert guidance in reaching a view, or at least developing scenarios, on the likely future pattern of service levels. We will discuss all of this in more detail later on.

Choosing between different forecasting approaches

A number of remarks can be made in order to ensure good practice in the use of models, whatever the model employed. First, elasticities are not usually linear. That is, demand does not respond uniformly to changes in factors such as price, or quality of service, throughout the range of possible values. There is usually an S shaped curve with demand growing rapidly, after a slow take-off, and then eventually saturating. Some modelling exercises mistakenly use linear relationships hidden in their mathematics.

Demand may also be subject to thresholds. Below a certain income level, for example, an individual may rarely fly, or at least fly only on low cost services. The functions adopted to describe demand also should not fall to zero but need to assume decay to a basic service level. The demand function should be non-linear with a fat tail rather than being linear falling to zero.

Calibration of model results is a very important part of the modelling effort. That is anchoring the forecast in real world performance. LAN, for example, compares survey data used in its modelling work with real operating data. Because of difficulties in collecting data, discrete choice modelling is sometimes based (at least partially) on stated preference surveys. These have the advantage of being able to explore issues of quality of service in great detail and they give a good picture of relative advantages and disadvantages. However, they are not a reliable guide to the absolute value of an investment, or other change. In practice, the experience is that changes in preferences are more extreme in stated preference responses than they are in real life behaviour. So one should not use stated preferences on his own to estimate elasticity, or other forecasting parameters. For this purpose the scale of stated preference needs to be adjusted (typically using joint revealed preference – stated preference estimation) and the constant terms need to be corrected.

Data is always a challenge. Data sources have changed as the aviation business changes. Data on ticket sales through conventional channels, as routinely reported by IATA, is no longer adequate as direct internet sales now account for such a large share of trips – 60% in Europe – and sales through tour operators and charter flights have always been absent from the IATA dataset.

The more disaggregated modelling exercises can require very large amounts of data that is difficult and costly to acquire. The level of modelling detail required to inform a decision should be considered carefully and aggregate elasticities are a reasonable substitute for behavioural survey data in some circumstances. Network Airlines tend to find it worth investing in detailed models and data as they need to understand markets at a disaggregated level. Airports and especially large airports will find it sufficient to model aggregate demand, with less data-intensive models. When using aggregate elasticities it is very useful to cross check results between models and across countries (the survey of research results by Gillen, Morrison and Stewart (2002), the analysis and discussion in Oum, Fu and Zhang (2009) and in InterVISTAS (2007).

At the most detailed end of the spectrum, discrete choice models have the advantage of being able to examine the entire end to end journey, including access to the airport of departure and the surface transport onward journey at the destination. They are particularly useful for examining intermodal competition, between air, road (car and bus) and rail and taking account of factors that determine quality of service (ease of access, convenience of transfers, inconvenience of transferring from public transport with luggage, etc.). Lufthansa has used discrete choice models for operations in Europe for some time. It uses them to optimise operations, with a culture of optimization reflected similarly in its unusually heterogeneous fleet of aircraft, designed to match market demand closely. EasyJet and Ryan Air at the other end of the scale do not model operations. Their business model is dependent above all on price competition and cost control, factors that do not require highly disaggregated modelling. When faced with assessing the impact of building a high speed rail station at an airport, discrete choice modelling is very useful.

In summary, any good model helps understand investment and planning problems, and helps distinguish short term from long term trends. It helps identify gaps and weak points in assessment. A good model is a map to help guide decision making.

Getting the best out of the models used

Getting the best out of the models will involve, as discussed above, some technical questions to do both with the selection of the right models (that is, those most relevant to the market circumstances of the airport under consideration) and also to do with the validation and interpretation of the results of those models, drawing upon expert advice. Experience shows that it is equally important to look carefully at issues to do with the governance and organization of the forecasting work.

Research evidence indicates that these issues pose a risk of material inaccuracies to forecasts. In particular, the work of Flyvbjerg and colleagues (Flyvbjerg 2009 for an overview) studied forecasts that had been prepared for transport infrastructure projects over a period of thirty years, and across a range of different countries. That they found a track record including inaccuracies is perhaps not surprising, given the inherent technical difficulties with long term forecasts. But two other findings from this research are important in the present context. Firstly, demand forecasts tended to be positively biased – that is, they were far more likely to over-estimate demand – and thus a favourable case for investment – than the reverse. And second, the researchers were not able to detect, over the course of the thirty years of data studied, much material improvement in forecasting accuracy – despite the advances which have been made in methods, and often in data, over this period. This lead the researchers to conclude that a material part of the observed inaccuracies in forecasts were not just technical in nature but reflected two other factors. The first of these are to do with various psychological characteristics that result in over-optimism, and over-confidence in relation to favoured projects. More specifically, the work of Daniel Khaneman and colleagues (Khaneman (1994) or Khaneman and Tversky (1979)) has shown how these kinds of psychological factors can lead to biases in economic forecasting. The second factor has to do with the incentives created by funding flows and the processes needed to secure project approval; together these can create incentives to strategically overestimate demand and to overstate the positive impact of an infrastructure project. In other words, planners and managers may have a different set of organisational goals to a concept of "the public interest" – as suggested by public choice theory – or may be unable to thwart the influence of special interest groups.

The guidance provided by even robust forecasting and risk management systems can thus be overturned by the incentives created by funding flows. For example, in cases where airport charges are subject to rate of return regulation there is evidence of over-investment and higher costs (see Oum, Zhang, and Zhang, 2004). Similarly, when part or all of funding for airport expansion is provided by government there can be an incentive for a planner or an airport manager to aim for maximising funding whenever the political and economic climate provides the prospect of funds being available. This is particularly so when funding is provided by federal or multi-national (EU) institutions as increased funding has no impact on local taxation. The local stakeholders then receive potential benefits at no direct cost. In the US the Federal Government aims to minimise this effect by producing its own forecasts of airport traffic, denying financial assistance to airports where their forecast differs from the FAA forecast by more than 10%. The quality of the FAA forecasts is therefore critical (and although they are solid enough they tend to be adjusted very often to track recent trends instead of employing long term scenarios to evaluate risk) and as with any such rule, the rule will be gamed and airport forecasts aligned to maximise their chance of passing the hurdle regardless of what local risk analysis might indicate.

Over-investment is frequent in such circumstances (Niemeier (2013) and Maertens (2010) for evidence on over-investment in airport capacity in Europe). And the research evidence suggests that these incentives are sometimes (and perhaps often) reflected in misleading forecasts (Flyvbjerg and COWI (2004) and Wachs ((1990) for evidence on transport demand forecasts more generally). Some evidence specifically on airport demand forecasts is provided by Niemeier (2013). In a case study for Hamburg airport, he finds that forecasts prepared by the airport in 1996 to assess the case for investment in additional capacity significantly over-estimated aircraft movements (by over a third for 2010, for example). In part, this seemed to result from inconsistent, and implausible, forecasting assumptions on aircraft load-factors. He also finds that there is some evidence of over-optimism in the forecasts for some other German airports. More generally, however, the Roundtable discussion noted that there is relatively limited rigorous evidence available on the ex post performance of airport demand forecasts (a point also noted by Niemeier (2013) and, for the USA, in an ACRP report, which concluded that this should be a priority for future research (ACRP (2007).

There is a useful conceptual distinction to be made in this discussion between the two potential sources of bias outlined above. The first is essentially inadvertent and is a bi-product of psychological factors – in particular over-optimism and over-confidence – which in some circumstances might be considered positively beneficial characteristics of senior decision makers. The second, on the other hand, is knowingly strategic, without any obvious associated advantages. Nevertheless, these two sources of bias can overlap – and may reinforce one another - within an organization or project team. The key point here is that the research evidence shows that these types of bias can be of material importance in practice. And, correspondingly, in order to make better forecasts we need not only to make technical improvements – as discussed in the previous section – but also act to reduce the potential impact of these "optimism biases".

What steps are best likely to achieve this? Flyvbjerg and colleagues have made a range of suggestions on this (Flyvbjerg (2009) for an overview); four of these seem particularly relevant to airport demand forecasting:

- First, it is useful to engage expert, independent peer review of the forecasting work (recognizing the familiar challenges of establishing effective peer review processes).
- Second, it is useful to benchmark forecasts against comparator literature (for example, as noted earlier, Gillen, Morrison and Stewart (2002) provide a survey of research evidence on price and income elasticity, InterVISTAS (2007) provides an overview and some comparators as does Oum, Fu and Zhang (2009). To some extent, benchmarking can be seen as an approach toward the concept of "reference forecasting" proposed by Lovallo and Khaneman (2003)
- Third, there should be transparency in the development of forecasts; for example, publication of methods, peer review comments, results and benchmarks – with the aim of engaging commentary and advice from the wider stakeholder and analytical community with an interest in airport demand forecasts
- Fourth, it would be useful to aim to make provision for ex post evaluation of how the forecasts have compared to out-turn in practice.

Drawing this discussion together suggests the following emerging conclusions on steps toward better forecasts; an overarching theme here emphasises the value which can be gained from blending together quantitative analysis - based on econometric and statistical methods - and qualitative analysis, drawing upon expert assessment.

First, it will usually be worthwhile to use econometric and statistical analysis, of the kind described above and elaborated in the Roundtable papers, to help understand – in quantitative terms – the key drivers which have shaped demand in the past; and then to use this as a starting point to forecast demand in the future. Decisions on the relative merits of time series or choice analysis should be shaped by an assessment – preferably guided by expert advice - of prospective market circumstances; but sometimes a two-stage approach will provide the best solution – using time-series econometrics to develop forecasts for a broadly defined market and choice analysis to develop forecasts for specific airports within this market (Airports Commission (2013) for an illustration of this kind of two stage approach).

Second, it will be useful to draw upon expert guidance, perhaps using formal elicitation methods (such as Delphi) to make best use of this expertise. Expert guidance will be particularly helpful in the choice of forecasting methods and in advising on scenarios for the future development of airline networks, and the implications of this for competition and service provision at different airports. And expert advice will also be important in the interpretation of the emerging analytical results and in the development of forecasts from these results.

Third, it will be important to constrain the risks of optimism bias. Here expert guidance on emerging forecasts – as described above - and independent peer review will be helpful, together with transparency and engagement with the broad range of stakeholders with an interest in the forecasts, and benchmarking of the forecasts to the existing research literature.

Finally, we need to recognise that however successfully all of the foregoing is carried out there are likely to remain material risks and uncertainties in even the best airport demand forecasts. The key issues which this raises are then, firstly, how these risks and uncertainties should best be measured, and in this way recognised, in the presentation of airport demand forecasts. That is, how we can be (appropriately) "more modest". And secondly, how these risks and uncertainties are best taken into consideration in the planning of airport infrastructure investment. It is to the consideration of these issues to which we now turn.

Dealing with risk and uncertainty in airport demand forecasts

The basic problem with airport demand forecasts has been the large surprises which have quite often arisen – with demand sometimes falling well below expectation (although occasionally, instead, with out-turns well above forecast). These surprises matter because airport infrastructure often (although not always) involves large irreversible investments, also with long lead times. This can mean that a big gap between forecast and out-turn either results in resources being wasted on under-utilised capacity or, alternatively, results in congested facilities which lead to delays and reduced service quality (with likely financial and resource pressures in either case).

The first part of this report discussed ways of tackling this problem by "making better forecasts" – that is, improving the quality and accuracy of airport demand forecasts. The discussion of the papers at the Roundtable suggested various steps – both technical and institutional – which together might help to bring significant improvements. But this discussion also concluded that, even with these improvements, there would nevertheless still remain significant risks and uncertainties. In other words, material risk and uncertainty appear to be an intrinsic characteristic of airport demand forecasts (at least for the foreseeable future).

In view of this, it wouldn't perhaps be surprising to find that a discussion of risks and uncertainties formed an important part of the presentation of airport demand forecasts. In practice, however, this is typically not the case. For example, a study of airport demand forecasts in the USA found that this is "an often neglected aspect of forecasting" (ACRP (2007). Furthermore, where risk and uncertainty is considered, the treatment is often relatively simplistic (for example, the presentation of rather arbitrary high and low scenarios alongside a central forecast – ACRP (2007). And, perhaps for this reason, the risk analysis is rarely used in investment planning (ACRP (2012) which notes, again in the context of the USA, that "high and low forecasts have little input into subsequent planning efforts"). The position in Europe seems to be essentially similar, Burghouwt (2007).

So there appears to be an important paradox here. On the one hand, risk and uncertainty are widely recognised to be an important characteristic of airport demand forecasts, with potentially important consequences. On the other hand, these risks and uncertainties are often not subject to serious analytical consideration, nor are they effectively recognised in investment planning. The discussion at the Roundtable suggested some reasons for this paradox, and also suggested some steps toward helping to resolve it. Essentially, the paradox is a reflection of a particular approach to infrastructure planning which frequently comes to be adopted – what we might call a "one-shot" approach. Flyvbjerg noted in his research on major transport infrastructure investment that, "often there is "lock in" or "capture" of a certain project concept at an early stage, leaving analysis of alternatives weak or absent" (Flyvbjerg (2009). A UK study similarly described this process as "starting from solutions rather than from problems" (Eddington (2006). Essentially, what happens in this "one-shot" approach is that the planning process quickly becomes focused upon a preferred proposal. This is then often subject to extensive testing (against traffic forecasts, financial performance, cost-benefit results, environmental impact, and so on), but with relatively less extensive consideration of possible alternatives. There are a number of well understood reasons why infrastructure planning might develop along this path (including some of the factors discussed earlier which facilitate "optimism bias"), and some suggestion that the traditional approach to master planning might have provided additional impetus in the case of airports (ACRP (2012) or Burghouwt (2007). In the present context, there are two relevant conclusions. The first is that once a "one-shot" approach has come to be adopted, then - actually - an analysis of risk and uncertainty doesn't really add much value in practice (other, of course, than to tell you that you shouldn't be using a one-shot approach). And, in line with this, the Roundtable discussion noted that the presentation of a wide risk margin on forecasts was sometimes not seen to be helpful to senior decision makers, or particularly welcomed by them. The second conclusion follows directly from this. In circumstances where there are material risks and uncertainties to forecasts then a "one-shot" approach to infrastructure planning is quite likely to prove less efficient than an approach which, firstly, aims to recognise risks and uncertainties. And, secondly, then uses this recognition as a basis for building into the infrastructure planning process ways of controlling, diversifying and reducing the (adverse) impact these risks. And thirdly, in this way, aims to improve the efficiency (and expected value) of infrastructure investment.

The Roundtable discussed how risks and uncertainties might best be recognised and (where feasible) quantified and how risk management measures might best be developed and their prospective value assessed. We will consider each of these in turn.

Recognising and quantifying risk and uncertainty

A key consideration in recognising risk and uncertainty in forecasts is whether or not we can reasonably assess the probability that a particular risk will materialise in practice. A useful conceptual distinction here is between, on the one hand, events where we have a pretty good idea of the chance (or probabilities) of different outcomes; and on the other, events where we have little realistic idea of the chances of the different outcomes or even, perhaps, what those outcomes might be (Kay (2009) for a discussion of these issues).

Events falling in the first group are most readily illustrated by games of chance; for example, whilst we don't know what score will result from a fair roll of a dice, we do know that the chances of getting a six (or any other pre-specified score) are one in six. Events like this are sometimes called "pure risks"; we don't know what outcome will arise in practice, but we do know the chances (or probabilities) of the different possible outcomes. And, correspondingly, we can work out the likely returns to different courses of action – different investment strategies for example – and make decisions in the light of this analysis.

Events in the second group are most readily illustrated by completely unforeseen catastrophes – the "unknown unknowns" – such as the Great Recession in the early part of this century or the influenza pandemic a century earlier. Events of this type are sometimes referred to as "Knightian uncertainties". Not only would it have been impossible to make any useful assessment of the probability of these events occurring immediately prior to their emergence, it's unlikely they would even have been considered as active possibilities. And in these circumstances, it is not possible to factor such events into decision making in any quantified or systematic way.

This distinction is thus rather important because the two different types of event have quite different implications in terms of how they are best analysed and recognised in airport demand forecasts. In practice, however, the events in which we are interested will often lie somewhere between the polar concepts of "pure risks" and "Knightian uncertainty", as we discuss in more detail in what follows. For this reason, Ian Kincaid and Nicole Geitebruegge decided to use the terms "risk" and "uncertainty" interchangeably in their Roundtable paper.

Quantifiable risks

The risks and uncertainties which are most readily quantified are those which are captured directly in the econometric and statistical models which underpin airport demand forecasts. (again see the Roundtable paper by Kincaid and Geitebruegge). Risk registers, examining the impacts of past events from the perspective of different parts of the airport business, are the first step in building risk awareness. For some variables, such as GDP, risk can be reflected in forecasts by looking at deviations from trend (recorded in historical data) and running the model many times (Monte Carlo modelling) to generate probabilities of deviation from the forecast in the future. This produces confidence bands around the central forecast.

Monte Carlo analysis has become much more accessible to general users thanks to the availability of specialised statistical software packages (ACRP (2012). In essence, the degree of precision which is achieved in tracking past trends can be used to assess the likely margins of risk and uncertainty associated with the model's forecasts of future trends. Of course, allowance also needs to be made for the similar margins of risk on the (input) forecasts of the key drivers of demand growth – e.g. future economic growth, fuel prices etc. Combining these various risks together, using techniques such as Monte Carlo analysis, enables a quantified margin of risk to be established around an airport demand forecast. Figure 1.1 provides an illustration of this approach – the chart shows a central forecast and also forecasting ranges which cover between 50% and 99% of estimated outcomes (ACRP, 2012) for a discussion of methods; this report includes some practical applications as does Airports Commission (2013).

Figure 1.1. **Illustrative prediction intervals**

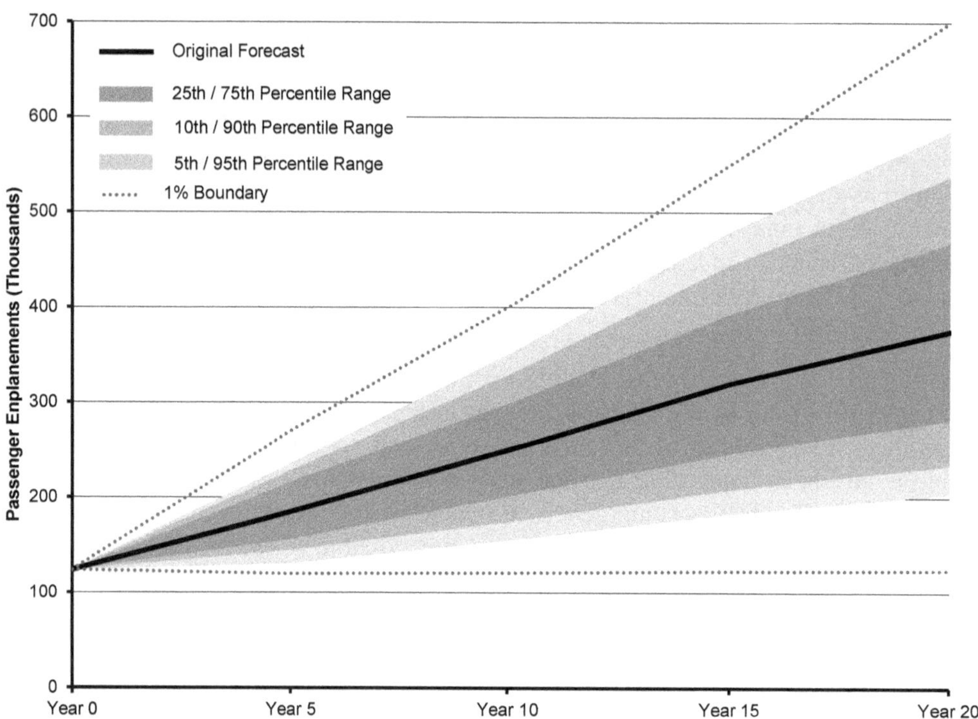

Source: "Addressing Uncertainty About Future Airport Activity Levels in Airport Decision Making", ACRP Report 76, 2012.

This kind of quantified measure of risk and uncertainty can prospectively be very helpful in making investment decisions (as we discuss further below). But we also need to recognise that what is being quantified here are the risks and uncertainties which are "in the model"; that is, in a sense, those which would arise "if the future were to look similar to the past". The question this raises is whether there might be changes in circumstances which lead to a materially different range of outcomes and, if so, how this should best be recognised in our forecasting analysis.

Subjective probabilities

In practice, there are a range of factors that might mean that "the future will look different to the past" – including changes in technologies and business models, climate change and associated policies, exceptional economic or social events, unexpected changes to consumers' tastes, and so on.

Whilst many of these risks cannot be "included in the model" – at least completely – not all of them are pure "unknown unknowns". In many cases there is a foundation of emerging research evidence and a body of expert opinion upon which to draw. This expertise might be best accessed using the kinds of formal elicitation techniques – such as Delphi – discussed earlier (ACRP (2012) for a discussion).

In some cases the research evidence may be considered sufficiently strong to formulate subjective probabilities of particular events (for example the prospective impact of developments in communications technologies on the demand for business travel). Again this provides a quantitative measure of risk which can be factored into investment planning, although a measure whose provenance is less secure than the quantitative analysis of past trends discussed in the preceding section. And other variables can be factored in according to the impact of specific events in the past.

In other cases, where the evidence is less strong, the research expertise might be used to develop scenarios – alternative future paths of development grounded in expert opinion – against which investment proposals can be tested Even though we can't say, with any useful certainty, what is the likelihood of the different scenarios the range of outcomes is useful in determining the spectrum of possible outcomes (Chapter 2 by Kincaid and Geitebruegge).

In some cases, the resulting projection surface may be so broad as to appear to give no guidance on future demand, but the exercise directs attention to providing capacity in as flexible manner as possible. Scenarios thus not only shed light on "how much" but "what kind of" capacity may be needed in the future. Even when Monte Carlo modelling and scenario analysis produces such wide bands that they are no use as a forecast, they do reflect the real risk and uncertainty that exists. This should be acknowledged, admitting that forecasting with precision isn't possible. And then using this analysis as a basis for developing methods to control risks, where feasible; and to reduce and diversify their adverse impacts, in the circumstances where the risk is realised in practice.

Unknown unknowns

Beyond this lie the pure "unknown unknowns". These are the types of event for which we cannot estimate any kind of probabilities, whether by using objective data analysis or subjective expert opinion. However good a map modelling provides, this kind of "Knightian uncertainty" cannot be incorporated, by definition. This kind of uncertainty concerns Nasim Taleb's Black Swan events, something never so far experienced. Such events simply cannot be factored into forecast scenarios as they cannot be defined. However, the process of building scenarios to map out the space bounded by quantifiable risks creates an appreciation of forecasts that prepares decision-makers for responding to uncertainty.

Scenarios can be built to test the sensitivity of central forecasts to upside and downside risks that can be identified, as described above. For example, although no one can predict the GDP in 10 years or regions of political instability in 20 years, scenarios can be built around the occurrence of deviations from long term trends in the past. Similarly the frequency of events such as outbreaks of new virus strains and their impact on travel can be modelled. And as events such as the outbreak of SARS and volcanic eruptions under heavily used flight paths occur, what were once Black Swans become more identifiable risks. Similarly, whilst economic downturns are regularly factored into scenarios, the size of the economic crisis of 2008 was unprecedented since the Great Depression and widely thought more or less impossible with today's financial institutions. Recessions of this scale are now likely to be factored into forecast scenarios as an extreme but plausible risk.

Risks more specific to aviation markets include airline bankruptcies and airlines moving hub operations out of an airport. What is of relevance in our present context – that is, forecasts for long term infrastructure – is the impact of these events over the medium/long term, that is, beyond the immediate shock effect. Thus, whilst origin-destination traffic tends to bounce back from shocks, transfer traffic does not usually return when an airport loses a hub operation. Examples include Zurich, Budapest and

Lambert St. Louis following the bankruptcies of Swissair and Malev and the decision of American Airlines to consolidate hub operations elsewhere.

In a world in which the number of hubs is probably likely to continue to fall (reflecting a range of factors including the legacies of the regulatory era and of early network development together with developments in both technologies and business models) then the loss of hub status is not usually recovered (Redondi, Malighetti and Poleari (2012). Such events are towards the more catastrophic end of the spectrum for airports. Unexpected entry can have a positive impact of a similar scale (Chapter 2 by Kincaid and Geitebruegge). Whilst, as noted earlier, research evidence to guide forecasts of the future development of airline networks and airport competition is still evolving (ACRP (2013), expert advice can be used to help analyse the problem in terms of scenarios.

This still leaves the pure "unknown unknowns" - events which may well not even be in the scenario analysis, because ex ante they wouldn't readily be considered. In a sense, there is not much that can really be done about this. However, event analysis could give an indication of the incidence of unforeseen incidents in the past and their impact, and particularly whether these impacts where essentially transitory or whether longer term in nature. Taken together, this might provide some indication of the potential importance of making provision for the unforeseen.

Drawing the discussion together, this suggests advantages to an approach which blends together the quantitative and the qualitative. An approach which first uses techniques, such as Monte Carlo analysis to get quantitative measures of the risks and uncertainties, which are "in the model", using econometric and statistical analysis of past data. But an approach which also recognises that a model which successfully fits the past may not equally fit the future, and which uses expert opinion – perhaps codified using formal elicitation techniques – to consider whether and how the model's forecasts should be re-interpreted. In some cases, there will be a sufficient research base to develop useful subjective probabilities to supplement, or substitute, those suggested by the model. In other cases, where uncertainties are greater, then expert opinion can help develop plausible alternative scenarios, even if it is not possible sensibly say which, if any, of these scenarios is most likely to happen in practice. (see, for example, UK Airports Commission (2013) for an illustration of an approach which uses both quantitative and qualitative analysis of risk and uncertainty).

In any event it will be important to be transparent about which risks are included in the quantitative analysis (and which are not) and the methods used to estimate these. And to be similarly clear about the use of subjective probabilities (and the provenance for these) and the evidence underpinning scenario development.

The main purpose of this analysis, as noted earlier, will be to help develop investment strategies which aim, where possible, to control, to diversify, and to reduce the negative impact (or vice versa) of risks and uncertainties - and in this way to improve the overall efficiency of infrastructure investment. This is the topic which we consider in the final part of this paper.

Before that, however, we will look in a bit more detail at one particular risk – future airline network development and the implications for competition between airlines and airports – which has been identified as a particularly important risk for airport demand forecasts (ACRP (2013) or Burghouwt (2007) and on which there was an extensive discussion at the Roundtable.

Airport demand forecasts and airline network development

As the development of Ahmedebad airport illustrates, many new airports have been planned as hubs, but it is airlines rather than airports that make the choice of where to locate hub operations. Heathrow serves as the hub of British Airways, while Copenhagen fulfils the same role within the SAS network. No network carrier operates hub activities at Gatwick, despite its 35 million passengers a year, while Copenhagen is a hub with half that number of passengers. As the markets of the United States and Europe have matured, and new airline business models, notably low-cost carriers, have become more important, then the number of international hub airports has decreased.

According to Redondi, Malighetti and Paleari (2012), 37 worldwide airports were dehubbed over the period 1997-2009. These airports did not recover their original traffic and dehubbing generally seems to be irreversible. When a network carrier stops operating hub activities at an airport it is not usually replaced by another network carrier but instead by low cost carriers (Redondi, Malighetti and Paleari (2012). This can leave airports with expensive infrastructure suited for transferring passengers but instead hosting low cost carriers solely operating point-to-point flights and looking for more basic infrastructure provided at low airport charges.

When planning a greenfield airport, such as Milan Malpensa, it is therefore usually advisable to focus on origin-destination (O-D) traffic rather than transfer traffic. An option is to include some flexibility in the design that allows for implementing infrastructure to support hubbing activities at a later stage (recognizing that greenfield airports are relatively unusual in Western Europe and North America, where expansion more usually adds to existing capacity).

Another important issue is what to do with existing airports in the region when opening a new one. Many examples have shown that when the new airport is located further from the urban area, airlines are reluctant to move (ITF 2014). Moreover, even if the existing airports are closed, or if airlines are forced to move, this might initially result in fewer passengers as a consequence of the longer travel distance to the new airport (especially if there are other alternatives available). If the new airport charges are higher than the old ones this might also lead to negative effects for both the airlines and the passengers. At hub airports, higher airport charges are likely to particularly affect transfer traffic as transfer passengers usually have viable alternatives through other hubs and are usually price sensitive.

As Redondi, Malighetti and Paleari (2012) concluded, competition among hubs can be fierce, even on the global scale, since airports located in different continents often compete for the same O–D markets – although switching costs (to both airlines and their passengers) and, in some cases, bi-lateral constraints can both act to dampen the strength of competition. Therefore, new (local) regulations, such as airport taxes, could affect hub competition on a much broader scale. Experts at the Roundtable agreed that a government policy aimed at forcing its national carrier to move part of its hub operations to a new airport would be a risk. Although dividing international connections between a country's two largest urban areas might seem logical from the point of view of establishing an immediate market for a new airport, economic network theory shows it is likely to be costly. Due to the existence of economies of density, scale and scope, a mono-hub-and-spoke network is usually more efficient than a dual-hub-and-spoke network. Spreading a hub operation of a single carrier over two airports within the same metropolitan area, generally turns out not to be feasible. The hub carrier will not be able to serve the same amount of connecting markets as would be the case with a single hub. By splitting the hub operation over more airports, the carrier will lose economies of density and is likely to lose market share in the connecting market because less connections can be offered. In addition, the carrier will need to duplicate at least part of its short-haul network at both hubs. Long-haul services can always be made more profitable by simply moving them from the secondary to the primary hub so long as slots are available (Burghouwt 2013). Furthermore, a government policy aimed at spreading an airline's hub operations over two airports would also run counter to passengers' preferences for using a familiar airport (as noted earlier, described as "airport inertia" in Hess and Polak (2006). Some similar issues can arise from regulatory constraints on hub development, such as slot regulation.

These conclusions are supported by recent research in the USA which studied airlines' choices in multi-airport regions (see ACRP, 2013). The research found that airlines prefer to concentrate services at as few airports in a market as possible. The benefits of service concentration at a particular airport – as outlined above – are regarded as central to the achievement of legacy and network airline business models.

Discussion remains about what would be the optimal scale for a hub. De Wit (2012) states that a particular hub's viability can only be defined within upper and lower boundaries. At the lower boundary, a minimum size of hub origin and destination (O&D) markets, in terms of population and prosperity, is required to guarantee the relatively high yield from direct air services at the hub as compensation for the lower yield from the indirect air services provided to transfer passengers. These transfer passengers need to be collected by short-haul flights, which are necessary to feed the profitable long-haul flights. The larger the hub the larger the indirect market that can be served, but at the upper boundary, hubbing comes with a growing average cost as the intensity of the connection waves increases. There do appear to be dis-economies of scale as operational complexity and vulnerability to interruption grows (de Wit, 2012).

In any event, network carriers sometimes face capacity constraints at their primary hub airports. They may therefore decide to open a secondary hub in order to accommodate market growth, referred to as overflow hubs (for example, we discuss the case of Lufthansa in the next section). In most cases, these overflow hubs lack any natural advantage in the origin-destination market compared to the primary hub. Therefore the network airline generally serves the smaller intercontinental destinations solely from the primary hub, while serving the large volume destinations from both hubs.

If total demand for these destinations allows for daily service from multiple hubs, network airlines can achieve advantages in frequency of service by synchronizing the flights to the same destination from both hubs so as to serve destinations at different times of the day (Burghouwt, 2013). It should also be noted that many of the current network carriers are the result of mergers. This means that bilateral agreements, historical ties to certain countries and airports (with some corresponding differentiation in passenger characteristics), and passenger preferences for a familiar airport together often play a role in sustaining multiple hubs, at least for a time. Finally, in some cases, the current hybrid aviation regime[1] may force airlines to operate long-haul services out of multiple hubs even if, from a network point of view, consolidation on a single hub is more attractive (Burghouwt, 2014).

Examples of European multi-hub network configurations

Although political pressure and pressure from labour unions, especially with merged airlines, have played a role, it is important to note that all the European multiple hub networks that have emerged are a result of the network carrier's strategy, rather than regulatory conditions imposed by governments.

The only possible exception might be Air France KLM's complementary hub strategy, as the Dutch government imposed a condition in the Air France KLM merger agreement that assured that KLM's hub in Amsterdam would not be dismantled in the eight years following the merger. Since 2012 Air France KLM has had full flexibility to adjust its network but it continues to operate more or less as separate airlines within one group, each operating their own hub-and-spoke networks. To some extent this reflects differences in traditional business and cultural ties to overseas markets between France and the Netherlands and associated differentiation in passenger demand characteristics (Burghouwt (2013), together, perhaps, with passenger preferences for a familiar airport.

A somewhat similar story holds for IAG in which British Airways continues to operate its hub-and-spoke network from London Heathrow, while Iberia does the same from Madrid. Here the complementarities seem to be even clearer. British Airways and London have a historical focus and comparative advantage with regard to the North American market, while Iberia and Madrid have the same regarding Latin American markets. Before the merger, both British Airways and Iberia individually operated a dual-hub-network within their home countries for some time. Due to capacity as well as regulatory constraints at Heathrow, British Airways decided to move part of its short haul network, as well as some international connections, to Gatwick. However, this "dual hub" strategy undermined the feeder system of BA's long haul flights at Heathrow and as a result it moved all its hub operations back to Heathrow. In looking at options for the expansion of airport capacity in the south east of England, the UK Airports Commission has concluded that a dual hub strategy would probably not be viable for either a carrier or a network airline (Airports Commission, 2013).

A similar story held for Iberia. It operated a Barcelona hub because of capacity constraints at Madrid; in addition political rivalry between the Generalitat in Catalonia and the central government in Madrid may also have played a role. However, as soon as additional capacity at Madrid became available, Iberia consolidated the entire hub operation at Madrid, dehubbing Barcelona in 2005-2006. Ever since, Iberia operates all long-haul services from Madrid and none from Barcelona (Burghouwt, 2014).

Lufthansa operates a multi-hub network constructed around its primary hub at Frankfurt; as many as five secondary or tertiary hubs can be identified. Three of them - Zurich, Vienna and Brussels - used to be the main hub within their national flag carriers' network before these were acquired by Lufthansa. Because of their historical extensive feeder network, potential differentiation in travel patterns (reflecting their differing historical trading patterns) and central geographical locations within Europe, they all retain a small 'natural' advantage, in at least some markets, over Frankfurt. Their network incorporation shows a similar, "complementary" pattern as Amsterdam and Paris (or London and Madrid), although to a far less pronounced extent as SwissAir and Austrian Airlines have become progressively consolidated into Lufthansa; and they similarly benefit from passenger preferences for a familiar airport. A different story holds for Munich and Dusseldorf which have virtually no unique networks compared to Frankfurt, but mainly play a role as 'overflow' hubs. As a result, only in markets with a high demand between Europe and long-haul destinations (such as New York JFK and Dubai), does Lufthansa provide a direct, non-stop service from both Frankfurt and also Munich and Dusseldorf (although the latter is a tertiary hub with only a weak feeder system, which in part reflects peak hour capacity constraints (Burghouwt (2013).

The development of the network of Europe's fourth largest network carrier Alitalia also provides some interesting insights. It has operated a hub-and-spoke network from Rome, but changed to a dual-hub network in 1998 when the newly developed airport Milan Malpensa opened. The original plan was that foreign airlines serving the existing airport Milan Linate would move their operations to Malpensa, making the latter the main international airport for northern Italy and leaving Milan Linate as more of a domestic, short-haul facility. However due to the fact Milan Malpensa is located 50 kilometres outside Milan, while Linate is only 10 kilometres away from the city, many airlines were reluctant to move. In response to this, the Italian government proposed to put in place Traffic Distribution Rules to achieve a shift from Linate to Malpensa. However, the European Commission rejected the government's initial proposals (on grounds of discrimination); furthermore, the municipality of Milan wanted Linate to continue to offer high quality European connections to its citizens. In consequence, it was eventually decided that some European flights would still be permitted to operate from Linate (Redondi (2013) for a more detailed account). This resulted in two consequences; first, passengers travelling between Milan and European destinations often preferred to use the more convenient (and familiar) Linate, thus diluting traffic on feeder flights to Malpensa. Second, some inter-continental passengers also preferred to continue to use Linate – connecting via a major European hub – rather than incur the higher access costs in taking a direct flight from Malpensa (Redondi, 2013). The result was that the disappointing performance of Malpensa services – among other factors – led to Alitalia withdrawing inter-continental services from Malpensa in 2008 to concentrate them at its hub in Rome (Redondi, Malighetti and Paleari, 2012). It is also interesting to note that traffic growth for the Milan airport system over the period was lower than for the rest of the Italian market, despite rapid growth at the third Milan airport – Bergamo – which principally serves LCCs. It seems possible that the unsuccessful attempt to establish a hub at Malpensa may have damaged market growth for the Milan airport system as a whole (Redondi, 2013).

Markets for airports in proximity to intercontinental hubs

Large, prosperous cities provide sufficiently large markets for direct long-haul service to other large cities that can compete with services via nearby hubs, particularly for business travellers. Such cities are also attractive for long distance connections from hubs abroad, especially where access to the national hub airport is constrained. The market may also be large enough to support hub operations for regional, medium-haul international flights. Whilst a national airline will not split its hub operations across more than one hub unless forced by capacity constraints, a foreign owned network airline might consider establishing a hub in a secondary airport if it provides access to the national market and is located in a geographically strategic location for its long distance routes. The possibilities available to such airlines depend on the conditions attached to air service agreements; granting access under such agreements to secondary airports may be less contentious than granting access to the national hub airport where competition with the national flag-carrier is more direct. Where airports compete for traffic, airlines determine their network structures on the basis of slot availability and relative prices and passenger demand characteristics. To model the decisions of airlines in developing hub operations is not straightforward, not least because there are relatively few research studies which have provided robust, generalizable evidence on the factors which shape network development (ACRP (2013) for a discussion and also evidence from a series of case studies in multi-airport regions in the USA).

In modelling the user benefits, the generalised costs of travel (monetary and monetised time costs combined) need to be compared for alternative routings. Better connectivity and higher overall benefits might be available through the growth of feeder services through a main hub rather than direct services from a new secondary hub. This can be a particularly effective strategy when the main hub is in a city with multiple airports and most domestic flights are operated out of one of the non-hub airports – a common pattern where a large new hub airport has been developed to replace an airport closer to the city centre where expansion was no longer possible (ITF 2014). Developing more feeder services to the hub, or reinstating long-haul flights at the older airport may be a cost effective alternative to developing a second international hub airport in a secondary city.

New aircraft technology - for example, the introduction of the Airbus A350 and Boeing Dreamliner that are designed to provide long-haul O-D services in smaller planes at lower cost or the Bombardier C series which has the range and fuel economy to provide hub bypass for thin, medium distance routes - may increase the opportunities for development of secondary hubs by decreasing the multihub market threshold by allowing the hub carrier to serve smaller markets profitably (Burghouwt, 2014), although these developments will also enable thinner routes to be added to existing primary hubs. Such changes are particularly difficult to predict, as discussed already.

Connectivity to affordable international services for passengers in cities distant from the primary national hub airport can be facilitated, in most cases, by increasing feeder services to the hub airport (as opposed to an alternative airport in the capital). The size of the O-D market, rather than the potential hub market, is what will determine the feasibility of a second major airport.

Airport capacity expansion in south-east Korea

Lessons from deregulation in Europe include a rapid rise in low cost carriers serving many new routes from secondary airports, both domestically and internationally. A similar development might be expected in Asia if deregulation continues. In these circumstances, many of Korea's smaller airports would likely see their number of direct international connections increasing. In order to assess the implications of this development, it would be useful to study the feeder network at Incheon in more detail to look at the final origins/destinations of its passengers. That is, it might well be the case that passengers who currently travel by train to Incheon before boarding an international flight would switch to a direct flight from a local airport if/when one is offered by a low cost carrier. This leads to diverted demand and will have direct consequences for the demand for airport capacity at the local airports. As such, there is then a question of how capacity expansion at these local airports would compare, as a solution, with constructing a new airport. This, in turn, is likely to depend on which types of airline are likely to demand more airport capacity.

European experiences suggest that it is unlikely that a full service airline would be willing to operate an intercontinental hub in the south-east region of Korea, as it would face a comparative disadvantage compared to competing full service airlines operating hub activities in Seoul (which provides the largest O-D market in Korea as well as the largest airport capacity).

As a result, it is quite possible that better connectivity and higher overall economic benefits would be achieved through the growth of feeder services through Incheon rather than direct services from a new airport in south-east Korea. In order to assess whether this is the most efficient solution, the overall (net) economic benefits of alternative routings need to be compared in the modelling.

Seoul is located only 330 km away from Busan and can be easily reached by high-speed train. Although it currently requires a transfer to subway or bus to reach Incheon from Seoul station, an extension of the high-speed line directly linking Incheon to the rest of the network is currently being built and is scheduled to open at the end of 2014. Consequently, passengers departing from regions such as Busan, Gwangju, and Daegu will be able to connect both more quickly and less expensively (compared to short-haul feeder flights) to connecting flights at Incheon International Airport.

Nevertheless, Korea's second largest city, Busan, currently faces capacity constraints as its runway only provides around 60% of the normal runway capacity both due to the proximity of mountains and because of the military use of the airport. Airport expansion could therefore be considered if demand forecasts show that there is enough local demand. It seems, however, more risky to focus on providing capacity for intercontinental transfer passengers. As mentioned above, the intercontinental hub operations of Korean Air and Asiana at Incheon airport, which can now be accessed from Busan via an efficient high speed train connection, makes it unlikely that any airline would be interested in operating a hub for intercontinental flights at Busan airport.

International experience thus seems to suggest that Korea's policy of focusing on the main hub and increasing its catchment area through better feeder services is likely to be more efficient than seeking to open a secondary hub. For example, in Europe both the Spanish flag carrier Iberia and its Italian counterpart Alitalia each operated a dual hub strategy across their two largest domestic cities for a while. However, in both cases it turned out to be rather inefficient, and commercially unsuccessful, and both airlines decided to operate a single hub in their capital cities. To put this into perspective, the distance between the cities is about 500 km in both cases, broadly 50% further than the distance between Busan and Seoul. The continued operation of complementary hubs in both Paris and Amsterdam by Air France - KLM tells a slightly different story, one driven by some degree of segmentation in the relevant markets (see Burghouwt, 2013) and, perhaps, the preferences of passengers for a familiar airport; as, similarly, does the case of the hubs operated by IAG in London Heathrow and Madrid. All of this illustrates the importance of a case by case analysis of market conditions.

Nevertheless, most empirical and theoretical studies have shown that concentrating activities on the primary hub is generally the most efficient policy from an economic and commercial perspective, a conclusion supported by recent research in the USA into airlines choices in multi-airport regions (ACRP, 2013).

Summarising, it seems unlikely that a full service carrier would be interested in operating an international hub in the south east region of Korea. On the other hand, as noted previously, European experience shows that low cost carriers might rapidly open new routes, as soon as the regulatory framework allows them to do so. This might suggest that expanding local airports located close to urban areas may provide better value, in economic terms, than building a large new airport in a less accessible area. This latter option could result in longer travel times to the airport, and lower demand, as well as higher construction costs, although local environmental impacts will also need to be factored into the equation.

Overall, south east Korea can be expected to provide sufficiently large markets to make viable direct services to other large cities, both domestically and internationally, that can compete with services via the hubs in Seoul, Tokyo and Shanghai, particularly for business travellers. These flights might be offered by Korean full service carriers as well as low cost carriers. European experiences have shown that in short haul markets low cost carriers can rapidly expand to market shares exceeding 33% in some instances.

In addition, if local demand in the region is sufficient then it is possible that foreign full service carriers – such as Emirates – might choose to offer long haul flights to both Incheon and south east Korea (as part of a strategy to offer a high frequency and capture high yield business class passengers).

Finally, the market may be large enough to support hub operations for regional, medium haul international flights. A foreign owned network airline might consider establishing a regional hub if it provides access to the national market and if it is located in a geographically strategic location for its long distance routes. However, the possibilities available to such airlines depend on the conditions attached to air service agreements. Granting access under such agreements to secondary airports may be less contentious than granting access to the national hub airport where competition with the national flag carrier is more direct. Where airports compete for demand, airlines determine their network structures on the basis of slot availability and prices as well as passenger demand characteristics. As noted earlier, however, there is at present relatively limited research evidence to underpin models of airlines decisions in the development of hubs and networks (see ACRP (2013) for an overview) and forecasts of this need to be based on alternative scenarios developed with expert guidance, not least because new aircraft technologies may well shift the balance of these choices in the future.

Airline network development and airport demand forecasts

Drawing this discussion together, the research evidence shows that levels of air service are often an important factor in shaping passengers' choices between different airlines and airports and can therefore be an important factor in shaping airport demand. But airlines' business decisions – which shape service levels – are less well researched or understood, particularly in relation to network development. The discussion at the Roundtable, both of research findings and recent experience, suggests the following emerging conclusions.

First, most theoretical studies of airline networks suggest that it is usually beneficial – in economic and commercial terms – for a network airline to focus its operations in a particular market on a single hub (and in this way get the best value – in terms of costs and service levels – out of exploiting density economies). Nevertheless, some studies suggest that a multi-hub network may sometimes prove more efficient, perhaps in situations where there is strong geographic segmentation between different parts of the market, together with sufficient O-D demand. And it is also possible that at high levels of traffic there might be various diseconomies of larger hub size which start to off-set the benefits of density economies.

Recent empirical research in the USA (ACRP, 2013) provides some support for these findings. In particular, the study found that airlines prefer to concentrate services in a particular region at as few airports as possible. The benefits of concentration at a particular airport are regarded as central to the achievement of legacy and network airline business models. Nevertheless, larger carriers will sometimes operate at more than one airport in a large metropolitan region if the demand conditions provide for this. More generally, the provision of airline services at alternative airports is usually found to be shaped by the suitability of these airports for the provision of niche services by low cost carriers. These carriers tend to focus on point to point traffic, and this means that they usually choose to serve a region through a single gateway.

Experience in Europe also supports these emerging conclusions, although in a slightly more nuanced way. This experience shows a number of unsuccessful attempts to establish dual hubs (in particular, Rome-Milan Malpensa, Heathrow-Gatwick and Madrid-Barcelona). This lack of success seems to reflect both the advantages of a single hub in exploiting density economies, perhaps coupled with passengers' general inertia in switching away from a familiar airport; and additionally ,in the case of Milan, competition from a well-established and highly accessible short-haul airport at Milan Linate. However, the European experience also shows a number of examples of legacy hubs – that is, hubs inherited from the regulated era – which have been successfully sustained in a multi-hub network (for example, Paris-Amsterdam, London-Madrid or Lufhthansa's configuration constructed around its primary hub at Frankfurt). The continuing success of these multiple hubs seems in many cases to reflect a degree of complementarity, with relatively strong geographic segmentation in their markets (typically the various partner hubs are located in different European countries with different historic patterns of trade and business connections, see Burghouwt (2013), perhaps also reinforced by passengers' general preference to continue using a familiar airport. However, in some cases – Lufthansa's secondary and tertiary hubs at Munich and Dusseldorf – their role seems primarily to offer direct services to only the most popular long haul destinations in addition to the primary hub at Frankfurt, in part reflecting the evolution of capacity constraints there (see Burghouwt's (2013) discussion of "overflow" hubs).

Finally, whilst our understanding of the factors shaping today's airline network development is incomplete – and often qualitative rather than quantitative – these uncertainties compound as we look into the future. It seems very likely that developments in technology will bring further changes. In particular, the introduction of smaller, lower cost aircraft (such as the Airbus A350 or the Boeing Dreamliner) on long-haul services, coupled with rising demand levels as the world economy starts to recover from the Great Recession, are likely to bring a greater role for point to point services, quite possibly provided from non-hub airports (although these types of aircraft will also support the provision of additional thinner routes from some existing hubs).

Developing and assessing risk management measures

As discussed in the previous section, the main purpose of recognising and quantifying (where possible) risks and uncertainties in future airport demand is to help to develop useful risk management measures. Thus the aim is not simply to tell us how risky and uncertain a proposed investment project might be; rather the aim is to help develop investment strategies which help to control and diversify adverse risks and to reduce their impact upon financial and/or economic returns (and vice versa for upside risks). And in this way, to improve the efficiency and added value of infrastructure investment.

The emerging evidence discussed at the Roundtable suggested productive ways of achieving this, and thus making airport infrastructure investment more robust to the risks and uncertainties in future airport demand. Approaches divide into two broad groups:

- The first involve risk sharing; the aim here is to facilitate the control and/or diversification of risk – in particular, through vertical integration.
- The second approach involves a flexible approach to infrastructure investment – sometimes called (variously) flexible strategic/dynamic strategic/adaptive planning; the aim here is to reduce the (net) costs of unexpected traffic outcomes.

We will consider each of these in turn.

Risk sharing and vertical integration

As the discussion in the previous section illustrated, an important risk to the demand forecasts for some airports – those which face a material degree of competition – is the possibility that key customer airlines may choose to re-locate their business to a competitor airport. This carries the risk of under-utilised – and under-remunerated – infrastructure. And this risk may, in turn, weaken investment incentives (there is of course a different, familiar, set of issues on investment incentives which arise in the case of airports which don't face material competition and are able to exercise market power; here the regulatory framework is a key shaper of investment incentives – ITF/OECD (2014) for a discussion).

In the case of airports which face a material degree of competition, the issues which arise are also found, to different degrees, in many other business settings. The essential problem arise where there is a need for large sunk costs – for example, in physical or human capital or in intangible assets – on one side of the supply chain. This situation raises the risk of ex-post appropriation, or stranding, of the assets. A common business solution is some form of vertical integration, with the aim of assigning particular risks to the parties best able to control the risk, or to diversify it ((for an overview: Kay, 1993). In most cases the form of vertical integration is more subtle than a simple "make-buy" dichotomy and may involve cross ownership (majority or minority), a classic contract or a long term relational contract (Kay, 1993).

In the case of airports, the regulatory reforms of the last several decades have both prompted and facilitated widespread innovation in organisation and ownership (see, for example, Gillen (2011) for a review). And these developing business arrangements quite often involve vertical relationships between airports and airlines (Frohlich, Muller, Nemeth, Niemeier, Njoya and Paskin (2011) for an overview and a discussion of the public policy issues which may arise from vertical links of this kind). In practice, vertical relationships take a range of forms. For example, David Starkie (2012) discusses the role of long term contracts (between airlines and airport), which have been used to manage some of the demand side risks to the development of major infrastructure by providing some control over the risks of asset stranding, at airports in a competitive market setting.

Another example is provided by the various different methods which are sometimes used to, in effect, co-finance airport development (Fu, Homsobat and Oum, 2011). And a further example discussed at the Roundtable is provided by Paris where probabilistic forecasts have been employed since 2003. Optimal points for new capacity, in terms of revenues and costs are determined. This provides the information required for informed negotiation with airlines that request increased capacity. When demand appears insufficient from the airport's point of view airlines can be asked to pay a risk premium if they want the airport to build early. This kind of risk premium can probably be hedged on financial markets. Some other airports are beginning to use this approach.

It is important to recognise that the benefits of vertical links may run wider than just the facilitation of investment in long term infrastructure at airports in a competitive market setting. For example, vertical links may be important to sustaining service quality in the face of unexpected adverse shocks (related to weather or to security threats for example), where trust and co-operation between different parts of the supply chain will often be important to sustaining service quality.

And, of course, it also needs to be recognised that long term vertical relationships carry the risk of anti-competitive restriction, where a vertical link might be used to raise the costs of market entry. There is therefore likely to be a balance of both benefits and costs to at least some vertical links. Competition authorities will need to be alert to this trade off, and the balance of benefits and costs will need to be assessed on a case by case basis. This will not be straightforward. However, the risks of an anti-competitive restraint will generally be greatest in circumstances where an airport has material market power, and this is also where the risks of expropriation/asset stranding are likely to be least strong (and vice versa).Transparency of vertical links will also be important (although not necessarily straightforward to achieve).

It also needs to be recognised that vertical relationships can only improve the control of risks which are endogenous to the aviation business (for example, the risk that an airline will choose to move more of its business to an alternative airport). Vertical integration won't improve the control of exogenous risks (for example, a downturn in the economy), although it might help with the diversification of such risks.

Flexible infrastructure investment

Whilst risk sharing can help to control, or to diversify, the risks associated with airport demand forecasts, a flexible approach to infrastructure investment aims to reduce the net costs of downside risks being realised in practice (or to increase the net benefit, in the case of favourable surprises). This approach has been variously described as adaptive/dynamic strategic/flexible strategic planning (Burghouwt (2007) for a discussion of the detailed differences between these concepts) and is particularly associated with the research of de Neufville and colleagues (see, for example, de Neufville and Odoni (2003).

The basic idea behind this approach is to seek to retain flexibility, either in the scale of the infrastructure – by holding open the possibility of adding to (or subtracting from) the intended capacity – and/or in the timing of the proposed investment. The aim of retaining flexibility in these ways is to help respond to unexpected traffic outcomes and, in this way, to achieve a better fit between the capacity provided and that which turns out to be needed in practice. The approach is sometimes described in a real options framework (Roundtable paper by Ian Kincaid and Nicole Geitebruegge). That is, an infrastructure project is developed in a way which holds open a series of options (essentially to do more or less) which can be taken up in response to changing circumstances (or not, if the central forecasts turn out to be realised).

Of course, flexibility of this type will usually come at a price. That is, holding open an option will usually add to costs. And it will usually, therefore, be less good value to do so in circumstances where the central airport demand forecast turns out to be accurate. The key question is then how much value is added by a flexible solution in circumstances where there are unexpected traffic outcomes; and whether these unexpected outcomes are sufficiently likely to occur in practice, such as to make the flexible option a good investment.

The discussions at the Roundtable suggested that a flexible approach can sometimes (and perhaps often) be worthwhile. The Roundtable paper by Ian Kincaid and Nicole Geitebruegge sets out a range of flexible solutions which have been successfully used in practice (Table 1.1 for a summary).

Table 1.1. **Flexible airport expansion solutions for addressing uncertainty**

Land banking	**Reserving or purchasing land for future development, to allow for the option of expanding the airport as traffic grows.**
Reservation of terminal space	Setting aside space within the terminal for future use. The space can be designed so that it remains productive in the short-term (e.g. using it for temporary retail that can be removed easily).
Trigger points / Thresholds	The next stage of development goes ahead only when predetermined traffic levels are reached.
Modular or incremental development	Building in stages as traffic develops. This avoids committing to a large capacity expansion. At the same time, the airport can respond to strong growth by adding additional modules.
Common Use Facilities/Equipment	Common gates, lounges and terminal space.
Linear terminal design and centralised processing facilities	Allows the greatest flexibility for airport expansion since it is the most easily expandable and allows flexibility in the face of changing traffic mix
Swing gates or spaces	Can be converted from domestic to international traffic (or between types of international traffic) on a day-to-day basis.
Non-load bearing (or glass) walls	As with swing gates, terminal space can easily be converted from one use to another.
Use of cheap, temporary buildings	An example is Amsterdam Schiphol's low-cost carrier pier.
Buses rather than fixed transit systems	The service is easier to expand, contract and redirect.

Source: Kinkaid and Guitebruegge (2014).

Thus while we can't accurately plot the future we can build in flexibility. Real option planning is what follows from an analysis of risk and uncertainty. Flexible design can include the use of "swing gates" and moveable partitions to direct flows of passengers between terminals and planes to different areas of the terminal to relieve crowding – allowing spare capacity in domestic terminal areas to be used by international passengers at peak periods, for example, and vice versa.

Terminals can be constructed in phases rather than as a single large hall and flexible taxiways can be designed to accommodate a wide range of aircraft. "Land banks" can be employed, reserving space for security facilities expected to be required in the future for example, but in the short term using the area for retail services so the space is used for profitable activity. Buildings can be designed to have floors added in the future when expansion is needed. Both are examples of "real option" planning analogous to financial hedging. Whilst initial construction costs are somewhat higher, expansion will be considerably cheaper, reducing construction costs over the long term. Adaptive airport planning is the only response to Black Swans.

Another approach to forecasting that helps respond to risk and uncertainty is to forecast the long term trend and track progress in actual volumes along the trend. Trigger points for expansion are reached as the volume reaches defined points along the trend, but the timing of when these triggers are reached is dependent on outcomes rather than pre-determined by the forecast. This approach is employed at the airports run by the Port Authority of New York (Zupan, 2012).

Thus flexible solutions include, in particular:

- measures which make provision for future development without, at this stage, making a commitment to expand
- measures which make provision for incremental development as traffic levels develop

- measures which make provision for switching facilities between different types of traffic (e.g. international and domestic)
- measures which make provision for different types of aircraft
- measures which retain flexibility in the start and/or completion dates for a project.

Whilst there is a wide menu of flexible solutions which have been found to work in practice (as summarised in Table 1.1) in order to be successful they will usually need to be tailored to the specific market circumstances (current and prospective) of the airport under consideration. As the Roundtable paper notes "there is no standalone method or tool that can offer the correct set of strategies". The Roundtable paper suggests an approach which builds upon current practice (where ACRP (2012) offers a series of case studies) and then uses expert advice from airport stakeholders and subject experts to suggest solutions which are feasible and relevant to the particular airport under consideration, perhaps using formal elicitation methods to structure this advice.

The evaluation of whether particular flexible solutions are worthwhile can involve qualitative appraisal - based on expert judgement – and this is sometimes sufficient to provide a clear conclusion. For example, the Roundtable paper discusses an assessment of whether or not to reserve land for a (potential) second airport for Sydney. The assessment is summarised in Figure 1.2. In this case, the expert judgement concluded that the option of reserving land would generally be worthwhile across different scenarios for traffic growth.

Figure 1.2. **Decision tree for second Sydney airport**

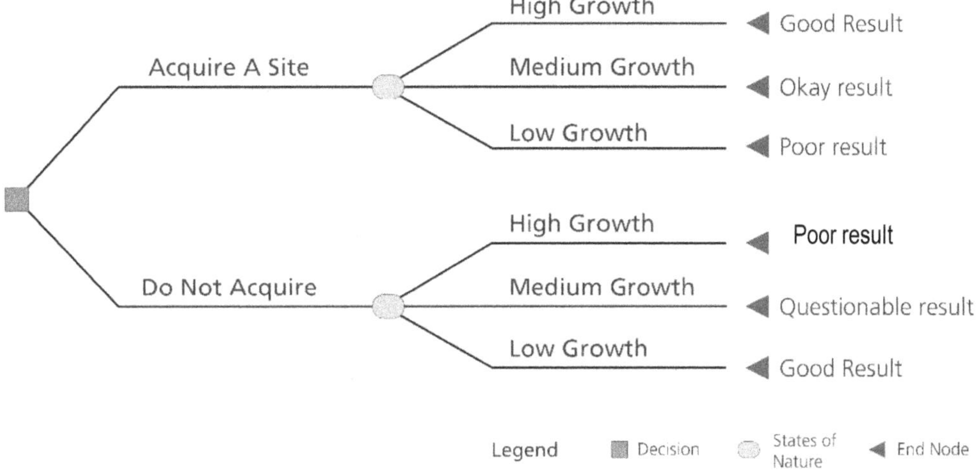

Source: Adapted from ACRP (2012).

In some cases a quantitative appraisal – which aims to measure the expected cost benefit return – will provide a more robust basis for decisions; although of course to do this requires some reasonable estimates of the probabilities of different scenarios for traffic growth (for example, using results from the kinds of Monte Carlo analysis described earlier).

Figure 1.3 provides an illustrative example of this kind of quantitative analysis. In the illustration, the non-flexible solution provides better value on the central traffic forecast. The flexible solution shows better value – in this illustrative case – when traffic levels are either well above or well below the central forecast. The key question is then whether the added value at the lower and higher ends of the forecasting range is worthwhile –in terms of outweighing the lower value which they provide on the central forecast; in the illustration, this is clearly the case.

Figure 1.3. **Example comparing probabilistic net present value**

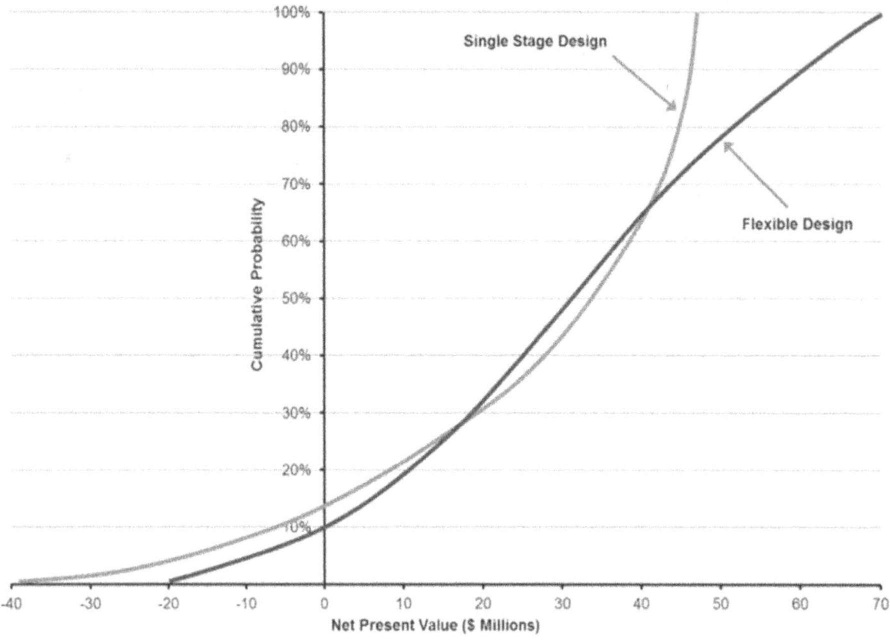

Source: After Kinkaid and Guitebruegge (2014).

Several case studies of the practical implementation of flexible infrastructure solutions in North America are documented in the ACRP report mentioned earlier (ACRP, 2012), whilst Burghouwt (2007) provides a detailed case study of flexible investment planning at Amsterdam airport. Although many of the examples of flexible infrastructure set out in Table 1.1 work at a relatively micro level – expansion of (a part of) an individual terminal, for example – the principles of flexible strategic planning can equally be usefully applied on a larger scale. For example, de Neufville (1995) considers the development of Amsterdam airport and the possibility of a new offshore airport; he judges this possibility to be an unwise commitment in a flexible planning framework.

More generally still, the UK Airports Commission are following an approach which might be characterised as an application of flexible strategic planning at the level of the whole London airports market. As a rule, flexible investment implies only building one runway at a time, building a second only when absolutely necessary. London's airports have maximised their return on investment in this way, by design or accident, and Gatwick carries 35 million passengers a year with just one runway. Airport building leads to higher charges, unless government decides to fund largely through general taxation. In other circumstances over-building will increase charges and that will depress demand and encourage passengers to use alternative airports. Athens' new airport provides a clear example of this effect.

In the UK, the Airports Commission has recommended that just one new runway be built to provide for growth in the London area, despite both Heathrow and Gatwick operating close to capacity, in order to keep prices competitive and contain the risks of over-investment. Conclusions on where to build have yet to be reached. Potential step-changes in airline behaviour are a key uncertainty. This includes the possibility of airlines relocating between airports and whether Gatwick could host a second hub operation in the London area. Expansion of Gatwick may represent increased flexibility. London benefited from its constellation of airports that evolved by accident more than design, as this proved very suitable for the entry of low cost carriers. Expansion of Heathrow would permit expansion of constrained hub traffic.

Note

1. The worldwide aviation regime is a mosaic of liberalized air service agreements, open skies treaties, regulated and deregulated national/regional aviation markets and traditional Bermuda-type air service agreements. For example, until EU-US Open Skies British Airways served Dallas, hub of its partner American Airlines, from Gatwick instead of Heathrow due to bilateral restrictions. For EU carriers, as long as the Community Carrier Clause is not accepted in all relevant bilateral agreements with non-EU states and the criterion of principle place of business has not been accepted in global air transport policy, carriers must rely on such traditional nationality clauses. These clauses limit the extent to which a multi-national airline can shift non-EU services between their European hubs. Finally, access to many markets is only possible by making use of hubs of alliance partners. For example, European network carriers can only access most cities in China by means of an alliance with Chinese carriers and creating connections through their hubs (Burghouwt, 2014).

References

Airports Commision (2013). Airports Commission: Interim Report, December 2013.

ACRP (2013), "Understanding Airline and Passenger Choice in Multi-Airport Regions", *ACRP Report 98*, Transportation Research Board. Washington,D.C.

ACRP (2012), "Addressing Uncertainty about Future Airport Activity Levels in Airport Decision Making", *ACRP Report 76*, Transportation Research Board. Washington, D.C.

ACRP (2007), "Airport Aviation Activity Forecasting", *ACRP Synthesis 2*, Transportation Research Board. Washington D.C.

Burghouwt, G. (2014), "Long-haul specialization patterns in European multihub airline networks – An exploratory analysis", *Journal of Air Transport Management*, Volume 34, January 2014, Pages 30-41.

Burghouwt, G. (2013), "Airport Capacity Expansion Strategies in the Era of Airline Multi-hub Networks", *International Transport Forum Discussion Papers*, No. 2013/05, OECD Publishing, Paris. DOI: http://dx.doi.org/10.1787/5k46n421b15b-en.

Burghouwt, G. (2007), A*irline Network Development in Europe and its Implications for Airport Planning*. Ashgate.

de Neufville R. and A. R. Odoni, (2003). *Airport systems: planning, design and management*. New York: McGraw-Hill

de Neufville, R. (1995), *Amsterdam multi-airport system: Policy guidelines*, Final Report for Amsterdam Airport Schipol. Cambridge, MIT.

De Wit, J. (2012), *The growth limits of the low cost carrier model*, Journal of Air Transport Management Vol. 21, 17–23.

Eddington, R. (2006), *The Eddington Transport Study*, December, London, The Stationery Office.

Flyvbjerg, B. (2009). "Survival of the Unfittest: Why the Worst Infrastructure Gets Built – and What We Can Do About It", *Oxford Review of Economic Policy,* 25 (3).

Flyvbjerg, B. and COWI (2004). Procedures for Dealing with Optimism Bias in Transport Planning: Guidance Document. London, Department for Transport.

Frohlich K, Muller J, Nemeth A, Niemeier H-M, Njoya E, and R Paskin. (2011). Vertical Structure of Air Transport: Problems for Competitio and Regulation. GARS Workshop, July 2011.

Fu, X., Homsobat, W., and T. H. Oum. (2011). Airport-airline vertical relationships, their effects nad regulatory policy implications. Journal of Air transport Manangement

Gillen, D. (2011). The evolution of airport ownership and governance. Journal of Air Transport Management 17 (1).

Gillen D., Morrison W. G., and C. Stewart. (2002). Air travel Demand Elasticities: Concepts, Issues and Measurement. Department of Finance, Canada.

Hess, S. and J. W. Polak. (2006). Airport, airline and access mode choice in the San Francisco Bay Area. Papers in Regional Science, 85(4).

IATA. (2008). Air travel Demand: IATA Economic Briefing No. 9.

InterVISTAS. (2007). Estimating Air Travel Demand Elasticities: Final Report

ITF (2013). Long run trends in travel demand. International Transport Forum, OECD Paris 2013.

Kahneman, D. (1994). New Challenges to the Rationality Assumption. Journal of Institutional and Theoretical Economics, 150

Kahneman, D and A. Tversky (1979). Prospect Theory: An Analysis of Decisions under Risk. Econometrica, 47.

Kay, J. A. (1993). Foundations of Corporate Success. Oxford University Press.

Kay, J. A. (2009). The Long And The Short Of It. The Erasmus Press.

Kinkaid, I. and Guitebruegge, N. (2014), Addressing Uncertainty in Airport Forecasting and Planning, InterVISTAS, ITF Discussion Paper 2014-10.

Koppelman, F. S. & Bhat, C. (2006). A Self-Instructing Course in Mode Choice Modeling: Multinomial and

Nested Logit Models. Washington, DC: US Department of Transportation, Federal Transit Administration.

Levine, Michael E. (1987). Airline Competition in Deregulated Markets: Theory, Firm Strategy and Public Policy. Yale Journal on Regulation, May 1987.

Lovallo, D. and D. Kahneman (2003). Delusions of Success: How Optimism Undermines Executives' Decisions. Havard Business Review, July.

Mason, K.J. & Alamdari, F. (2007). EU network carriers, low cost carriers and consumer behaviour: A Delphi study of future trends. Journal of Air Transport Management, Volume 13, Issue 5. The Air Transport Research Society's 10th year Anniversary, Nagoya Conference, 2006.

Oum, T. H., X. Fu and A. Zhang. (2009). Air Transport Liberalisation and its Impacts on Airline Competition and Air Passenger Traffic, ITF 2009 Forum, Forum Papers.

Oum, T. H., A Zhang and Y Zhang. (2004). Alternative Forms of Economic Regulation and their Efficiency Implications for Airports. Journal of Transport Economics and Policy, Volume 38, Part 2 217-246

Redondi, R.,Malighetti, P., Paleari, S. (2012) De-hubbing of airports and their recovery patterns, Journal of Air Transport Management, Volume 18, Issue 1, January 2012.

Redondi, R., (2013). Traffic distribution rules in the Milan airport system: effects and policy implications. Journal of Transport Economics and Policy 47 (3), 493-499.

Sallier, D. (2010). Long term demand forecast: the Kenza approach. The 2010 Air Transport Research Society Conference in Porto.

Small, K.A. and E.T. Verhoef (2007), The Economics of Urban Transportation, Second Edition, London and New York: Routledge.

Smyth A and G Christodoulou (2011). Maturity in the Passenger Airline Industry? Revisiting the Evidence and Addressing Maturity in Forecasting the Future Market for Air Travel. University of Westminster; available online

Starkie, D. N. (2012). European airports and airlines: Evolving relationships and the regulatory implications. Journal of Air Transport Management; Volume 21

Wachs, M. (1990). Ethics and Advocacy in Forecasting for Public Policy. Business and Professional Ethics Journal, 9

Zupan, J. (2013) Upgrading to World Class: The Future of New York Region's Airports. Discussion Paper 2013-1, International Transport Forum, OECD Paris 2013.

Chapter 2. Addressing uncertainty in airport forecasting and planning

Ian Kincaid and Nicole Geitebruegge[1]

This chapter summarises the research and results of a study conducted by InterVISTAS Consulting and sponsored by the Transportation Research Board examining how risk and uncertainty can be addressed in airport traffic forecasting and airport planning. The research developed a unified systems analysis framework that enables airport activity forecasters to identify risk factors, to understand the extent to which each risk factor introduces uncertainty into activity forecasts, and to ascertain how the risks and uncertainties are likely to interact so as to examine realistically their combined implications for air traffic going forward. Airport planners can apply the systems analysis methodology at different levels of quantitative and qualitative detail ranging from almost no quantitative analysis at all to highly sophisticated statistical and simulation based methods. This should make airport forecasting and planning more robust to uncertainty and risk although it is acknowledged that further research is required, particularly to more fully and formally integrate political risk into the systems analysis methodology.

1. InterVISTAS Consulting

Introduction

Forecasts of future airport activity are an essential tool for airport planning and financing decisions providing guidance on future passenger, cargo and aircraft activity that the airport may face and thus help define future facility, commercial and financing requirements. An accurate forecast used to drive investment policy creates significant value for the airport and its users. However, in recent years the ability of traditional forecast techniques to produce reliable estimates has come into question. There are numerous examples of unforeseen events and developments that led to dramatic and unexpected shifts in air traffic levels at some airports. An inaccurate forecast can result in poor timing of investment and lock in higher operating and financing costs. While some airports have experienced negative changes in airport activity, others have experienced unexpected strong growth, placing pressure on airport resources.

Nevertheless, many airports still rely on traditional forecasts to guide their planning and decision making. Generally, the only recognition of uncertainty is the development of low and high forecasts. However, these are generally produced as an afterthought with little attention given to drivers of uncertainty. It is also often the case that these low and high forecasts are given little attention in the planning process.

One of the challenges of the traditional forecast approach is that it typically treats uncertainties in the future as minor perturbations to the general trend line (as expressed through low and high scenarios). In reality, few airports find their actual traffic matches these trend forecasts, either in the long-term level of traffic or in the timing at which traffic reaches the critical levels requiring new capacity. Both the level and timing of future traffic is uncertain, and investment decisions based on steady trends can lock in airport costs and service levels in unwanted ways.

Our research examined the theory and practice of addressing uncertainty in the airport industry and in other sectors of the economy. Based on this research, a methodological framework was developed designed to augment standard master planning and strategic planning approaches. The framework provides tools for improving the understanding of risk and uncertainty in air traffic forecasts as well as tools for increasing the robustness of airport planning and decision making.

A critical conclusion of the research was that forecasting should consider "what can happen" and not only "what is most likely to happen". A less prescriptive but more informative forecasting methodology, considering the type, range and potential impacts of different risk and uncertainties that the airport is facing, can be an effective way to address risk and uncertainties and respond accordingly.

Sources of uncertainty and risk

Uncertainty about future airport activity levels can manifest itself in two fundamental ways:

- The overall **volume of traffic**: total passengers, total aircraft operations, air cargo volumes, etc., and their volatility over time.
- The **mix or type of traffic** at the airport: domestic vs. international, origin/destination (O-D) vs. connecting, low-cost carrier vs. full service/legacy carrier, turboprop vs. regional jet vs. large jets, etc.

In either case, there can be profound implications for the development of airport facilities and operations and can include both threats and opportunities. For example, declines in total passenger traffic can lead to facilities that are under-utilised with high operating and capital costs, supported by a too small traffic base. On the other hand, the sudden growth of international traffic could require the airport to enhance its facilities for processing international traffic such as immigration control, customs inspections, security processes.

Uncertainty in the volume and mix of airport activity stems from various sources; some are fairly global while others are specific to the airport in question. They can be grouped within the following categories:

- **Macroeconomic**: events in the general economy which can have implications on air traffic, such as a national recession, demographic changes (e.g. aging population), or more localised events such as the loss of a major employer.
- **Market**: events impacting the supply of, and/or demand for, aviation services in the airport catchment area. For example, entry of a new carrier, loss of an incumbent carrier, airline mergers, emergence of a new airport in the region, etc.
- **Regulatory/policy**: changes in regulations and rules governing the activities of airlines and/or airports. This can also include new environmental regulations on noise or emissions or the introduction of cap and trade policies.
- **Technology**: innovations that may influence the supply of and demand for airport services, such as new aircraft models that reduce the cost of air travel and open up opportunities for new routes.
- **Social/cultural**: changes in the attitude of society and business towards the use and value of air travel, e.g. use of internet technologies to conduct meetings rather than face-to-face meeting requiring air travel.
- **Shocks events**: unpredictable, infrequent events with potentially significant impacts (wars, terrorist attacks, geopolitical instability, etc.).
- **Statistical or model**. Forecasts of future airport activity are based on analytical models. Such models can be mis-specified (i.e., they do not correctly represent the underlying relationships) or subject to estimation error. Also, the historical relationships captured in the model may not continue into the future due to structural changes in the market.

Examples of the impact of uncertainty on airports

The following case studies provide examples where unforeseen events and changing conditions, not accounted for in the original forecasts, had a significant impact on an airport, either positive or negative. These examples illustrate the difficulties airports face as a result of air traffic uncertainty.

Case study 1: Hungary/Malév

Hungary joined the European Union in 2004, which resulted in the country becoming part of the highly liberalised European aviation market. At the time, the country's home carrier was Malév Hungarian Airlines, a state-owned airline which went through a modernisation process in the 1990s and 2000s. The airline was based in Budapest and primarily served destinations in Europe, Russia and the Middle East. In 2007, the government sold its shares of the airline to a private company. By 2010, Malév was in extreme financial difficulty due in great part to the severe recession that Hungary experienced between 2008 and 2010 (the country's GDP declined by 6.3% in 2009 alone). Even though the government attempted to save the airline through a substantial investment in the airline, Malév's had to cease operations in February 2012.

At the time of its collapse, Malév accounted for approximately 40% of passenger traffic at Budapest airport. However, there was a surprisingly rapid response to Malév's collapse by other carriers in Europe. Within seven hours of Malév's demise, Ryanair announced 31 new routes to and from Budapest. One of the reasons Ryanair was able to move so quickly is because it routinely parks some of its fleet during the winter low. A few days later Ryanair confirmed that the airline would operate a base from Budapest. A number of other airlines quickly announced new routes or additional capacity to/from Budapest including the Hungarian low cost carrier Wizz Air, Air Berlin, SmartWings and Lufthansa. Within just one week of Malév's collapse, 60% of the airline's lost capacity was replaced by other carriers. However, virtually all of the recovered capacity has been for EU destinations. Capacity recovery has been much slower (or has not occurred) on routes outside the EU, where the bilateral arrangements do not allow rapid changes in carriers including Russia, Turkey, Israel and the Ukraine. In addition, the airport has lost most of the 1.5 million in transfer passengers that it used to handle.

Budapest airport, which is privately owned and operated, has acted aggressively to attract other airlines to fill the services lost by Malév. The airport used to operate Terminal 1 for low cost carriers, and Terminal 2 (newly renovated and expanded) for Malév and other network carriers. Since Malév's demise, the airport has closed Terminal 1 and consolidated all operations at Terminal 2.

Case study 2: Zurich Airport and Brussels Airport

Zurich Airport (ZRH) served as the hub for Swissair, former national carrier of Switzerland. Due to its central position in Europe, Swissair (and thus ZRH) profited from generating transfer passengers. However, with the deregulation and liberalization of the air industry in the European Union (which Switzerland participated in despite not being a member of the EU) and the economic downturn during 2000 and 2001, Swissair experienced severe financial difficulties leading to the airline filing for bankruptcy in October 2001. Many of Swissair assets were taken over by a subsidiary of Swissair, changing the name to Swiss International Air Lines. As a result of restructuring, Swiss International Air Lines cut its seat capacity at ZRH by 43% between 2000 and 2004. The airline was subsequently taken over by Lufthansa (in 2007) but continues to operate as a separate brand.

The capacity cuts by its home carrier contributed to a 25% decline in total traffic at ZRH between 2000 and 2004 (Swissair accounted for 66% of traffic before its failure). In the years following, traffic gradually recovered (by 5.4% per annum), to almost reach its pre-collapse levels by 2008. However, the restructuring had a major impact on transfer traffic at ZRH. In 2002, the year following the collapse, total O-D traffic (i.e., to/from Zurich) was 12% below 2000 traffic levels, but transfer traffic had declined by 32%. By 2005, O-D traffic had recovered to 2000 levels while transfer traffic had declined by 48%. (Source: http://www.zurich-airport.com/the-company/zurich-airport-ag/statistical-yearbook)

A similar story occurred at Brussels Airport (BRU) which was the primary hub of Sabena, the former national carrier of Belgium. In fact, the two events are connected as it was the failure of Swissair to make a scheduled payment of USD 200 million to Sabena in 2001 that triggered Sabena's collapse. In November 2001, Sabena ceased operations, and many of its assets were transferred to a short-haul subsidiary, Delta Air Transport. In early 2002, the airline was renamed SN Brussels Airlines. The new airline cut seat capacity by 68% between 2001 and 2002. In 2007, the airline merged with Virgin Express and was renamed Brussels Airlines.

The airport experienced a 33% decline in traffic between 2000 and 2002 (Sabena accounted for 55% of traffic before its failure), after which traffic grew by 4.3% per annum so that by 2008 passenger traffic levels were 21% below its pre-collapse levels.

Both airports saw traffic decline dramatically, which was then followed by recovery. Even though some recovery has occurred, both airports are way off the traffic trend that was apparent prior to the airline failure.

Despite the loss of traffic following Swissair's collapse, ZRH decided to continue expansion plans which had started in 2000. In September 2003, ZRH completed its new Dock E. As a consequence, ZRH had considerable excess capacity. The lack of traffic led to a closure of the existing Dock B in the same year. As an example of adapting facility use, Dock B was converted into an event venue (EventDock) for a period of time, although it is now being reconstructed and was reopened in December 2011.

BRU had started construction of a new pier (Pier A) before the collapse of Sabena, which was completed in May 2002. Following Sabena's collapse, the decision was made to close the satellite terminal which had originally served as the terminal for the intercontinental operations of the airline.

Case study 3: Lambert-St. Louis International Airport

In 1982, Trans World Airlines (TWA) made Lambert-St. Louis International Airport (STL) its principal domestic hub which resulted in passenger traffic at the airport almost doubling between 1981 and 1986 from 5.3 million to 10.0 million enplaned passengers. During the 1990s, TWA drove strong traffic growth again, with total enplanements at the airport reaching 15.3 million passengers in 2000, despite the carrier entering bankruptcy protection twice (in 1992 and 1995). Connecting traffic accounted for a large proportion of passenger volumes during this period.

In response to this growth, a 1994 airport master plan update for STL proposed the construction of a third runway. The new runway was expected to allow STL to reduce delay times (which the airport had become prone to), improve adverse weather capabilities, enhance capacity, and continue to accommodate TWA's hubbing operations. This recommendation was supported by FAA Terminal Area Forecasts around that time, which predicted that traffic would reach 20 million enplaned passengers by 2006 and 25 million by 2012.

In early 2001, TWA again experienced financial difficulties, which resulted in its assets being acquired by American Airlines' (AA) parent company (AMR Corporation), and the airline declared bankruptcy for a third time. Following the severe downturn in traffic that followed the terrorist attacks of 9/11, AA began reducing its STL operations, focusing more on its main hub operations at Chicago O'Hare and Dallas/Fort Worth. In 2003, AA converted many routes to regional services, resulting in a significant loss of total capacity.

As a result, passenger volumes at STL declined by 56% between 2000 and 2004 to 6.7 million enplanements. Traffic failed to recover significantly from this level and declined further between 2008 and 2010 as result of economic conditions and further cutbacks by AA. The cutbacks by AA were somewhat offset by Southwest Airlines, which increased operations at the airport in 2010 and is now the largest carrier at STL in terms of departures.

Due to delays in the planning process, construction of the proposed third runway did not start until 2001. While some consideration was given to delaying the construction, given the uncertainty regarding the operations of TWA/AA, it was decided to continue development. This decision was supported by the FAA on the basis of enhancing national system capacity. During the period of construction, FAA continually revised its forecasts for STL enplanements downward. By the time the FAA completed its forecasts for 2003, it was projecting STL's passenger traffic in 2015 would be less than levels achieved in 1993. In fact, traffic continued to decline even further (Figure 2.1)

Figure 2.1. **Actual and forecast total passenger enplanements at Lambert-St. Louis International Airport**

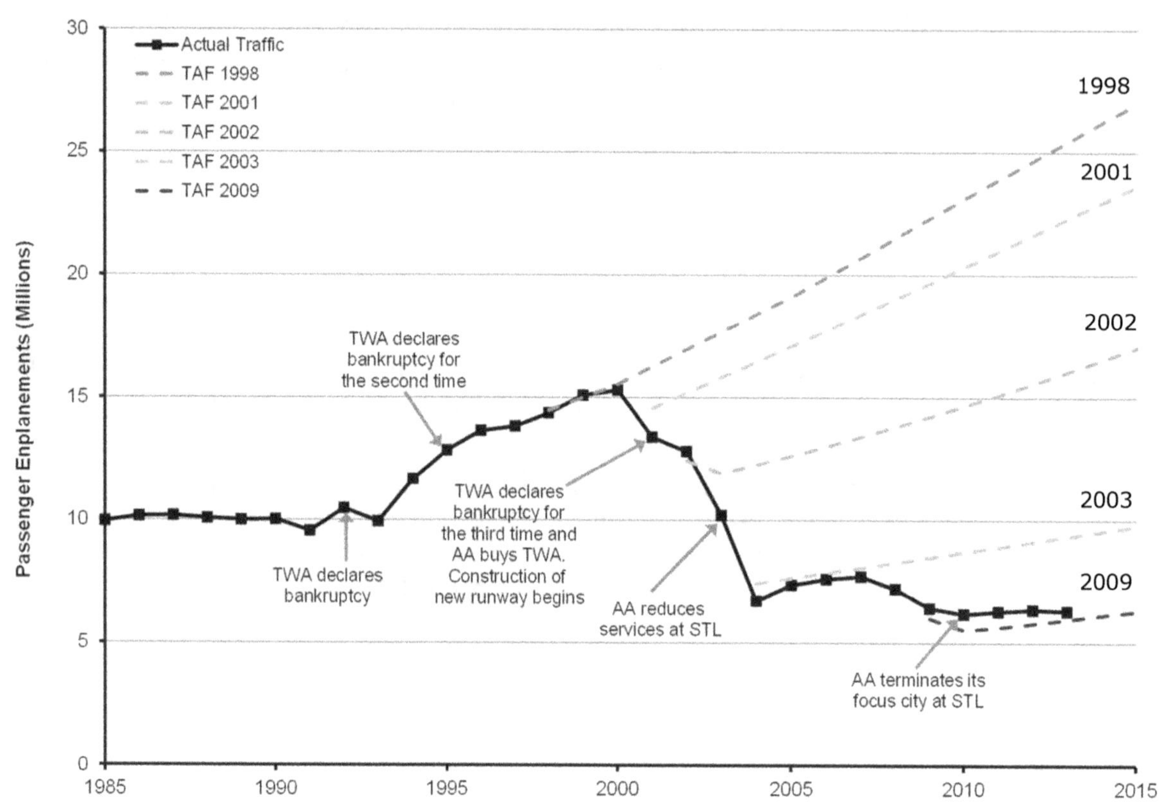

Source: ACRP Report 76, 2012.

Case study 4: Bellingham International Airport

Bellingham International Airport (BLI) is located in the state of Washington, three miles northwest of Bellingham, a city with a metropolitan population of approximately 200 000. The airport is approximately 21 miles south of the Canadian border and 90 miles north of Seattle.

Prior to the 9/11 terrorist attacks, BLI had service to Seattle operated by Horizon Air and United Express/SkyWest, accounting for 79% of their total seat capacity in 2000, plus service to the San Juan Islands off the coast of Washington. In October 2001 the United Express/SkyWest services were terminated, in part due to service rationalization following the 9/11 attacks. Traffic declined to a low of 64 000 in 2003. In August 2004, low-cost carrier Allegiant Air entered the market at BLI and started service to Las Vegas. Over the next few years, the airline increased the range and frequencies of service operated out of BLI. By January 2008, Allegiant Air opened up a base at BLI. By 2011, the airline operated direct service to six destinations. As a result of Allegiant's entry, traffic at BLI increased by 374% between 2004 and 2010, an average growth rate of nearly 30% per annum. Since the entry of Allegiant, traffic levels have greatly exceeded forecasts produced by the FAA and in the airport's 2004 master plan (Figure 2.2).

BLI's expansion plans were affected by the rapid and unexpected increase in traffic. For example, the expansion of the terminal building, originally scheduled to be completed in 2018, has been accelerated to be completed by 2013. In addition, a USD 29 million runway resurfacing project was completed in September 2010 which will enable larger aircrafts to operate at BLI.

This BLI example shows that upside risk can lead to a need for rapid airport expansion, in order to keep airlines and passengers satisfied, to ensure that airlines can continue to expand their services and to avoid congestion which may lead to a loss of passengers or the exit of a carrier.

Figure 2.2. **Actual and forecast total passenger enplanements at Bellingham International Airport**

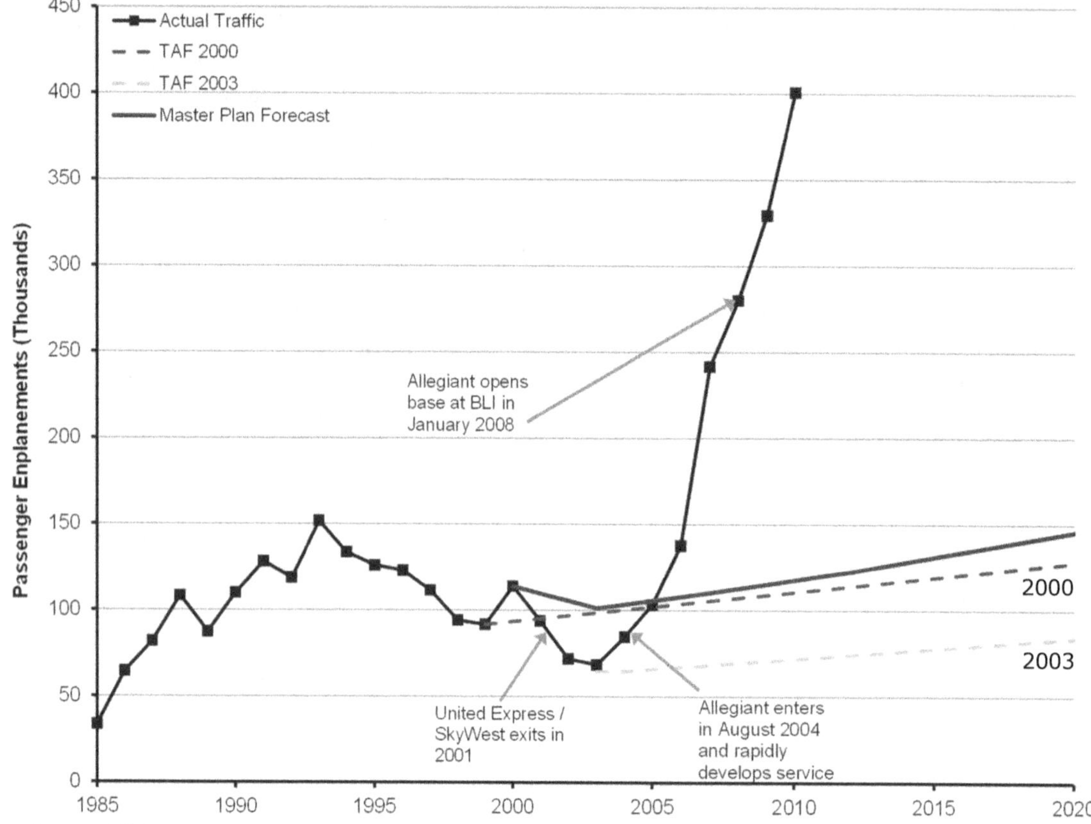

Source: ACRP Report 76, 2012.

Methods for better addressing uncertainty in forecasting and planning

As noted previously, the normal approach to addressing uncertainty in air traffic forecasting is to supplement the base case forecasts with high and low forecasts. These do convey that there is uncertainty in the forecast and provide a rough, although typically narrow range of likely outcomes. Other standard approaches include the use of "what-if" analysis, which generally looks at the impact of a single event, and sensitivity analysis, which examines the impact of varying key assumptions or model parameters.

However, these approaches provide airport planners and investors only a cursory understanding of the risk profile facing the airport and offer little information on the various factors that might influence traffic development. Furthermore, due in part to the limited insight they provide, the findings from these approaches are rarely incorporated into the planning process in any meaningful way.

Looking at the state-of-the-art revealed that additional helpful methodologies exists nowadays which can be used in air traffic forecasting to provide richer information on the implications of risk and uncertainty. Those methodologies can provide information to feed directly into the planning process and will depend on the needs and resources of the airport, but may include:

- **Delphi or Formal Elicitation Methods**. These are broad set of techniques incorporating input from subject matter experts and stakeholders, which allow risk factors to be identified and their impacts explored.

- **Scenario analysis.** A large number of separate scenarios can be developed and "played out" to assess the impact of different sets of events occurring together. These scenarios can be built on the findings from the Delphi/elicitation methods.
- **Monte Carlo.** A statistical simulation technique which makes use of randomization and probability statistics to generate an often wide range of possible traffic outcomes and provide estimates of the probabilities of such outcomes. Monte Carlo analysis has become much more accessible to general users thanks to the availability of specialised statistical software packages.

These forecasting approaches are not necessarily intended to produce more accurate forecasts; they are designed to provide a greater understanding and awareness of future uncertainty. This understanding can then be used in the planning process, as well as providing input to strategic analysis and financial analysis.

Furthermore, enhanced forecasting techniques provide the greatest value when combined with a planning process that seeks to achieve maximum flexibility in the face of an uncertain future. A number of conceptual and practical approaches have been developed in airport master and strategic planning which allow greater flexibility and diversification. Many of these approaches come under the umbrella of real options. Like financial options, a real option is the right, but not the obligation, to take a certain course of action. Real options apply this approach in the real, "physical" world rather than the financial world (although real options still have financial implications). The concept started to develop in the 1970s and 1980s as a means to improve the valuation of capital-investment programs and offer greater managerial flexibility to organizations. Real options and real options analysis is used in many industries, particularly those undertaking large capital investments, e.g., oil extraction and pharmaceutical.

The use of real options and its related analytical techniques is not prevalent as a concept in airport planning and design. However, some of the design choices made by airports do encapsulate the ideas behind real options. Examples of real options or flexible airport planning include:

- **Land banking** – reserving or purchasing land for future development, to allow for the option of expanding the airport as traffic grows.
- **Reservation of terminal space** – similar to land banking, this involves setting aside space within the terminal for future use (e.g., for security processes). The space can be designed in such a way that it remains productive in the short-term (e.g., using it for retail which can be removed easily).
- **Trigger points/Thresholds** – the next stage of development goes ahead only when predetermined traffic levels are reached.
- **Modular or incremental development** – building in stages as traffic develops. This avoids the airport committing to a large capacity expansion when it is uncertain when and how the traffic will develop. At the same time, the airport can respond to strong growth by adding additional modules.
- **Common use facilities/Equipment** – e.g., CUTE, CUSS, common gates, lounges and terminal space.
- **Linear terminal design and centralised processing facilities** - allows the greatest flexibility for airport expansion since it is the most easily expandable in different directions and allows flexibility in the face of changing traffic mix.
- **Swing gates or spaces** – can be converted from domestic to international traffic (or between types of international traffic) on a day-to-day basis.

- **Non-load bearing (or glass) walls** - as with swing gates, terminal space can easily be converted from one use to another.
- **Use of cheap, temporary buildings** - allows the airport to service one type of traffic (e.g., low-cost carriers) while keeping options open to serve other types (e.g., full service or transfer). An example is Amsterdam Schiphol's low-cost carrier pier.
- **Self-propelled people movers (e.g., buses) rather than fixed transit systems** – the service is easier to expand, contract and redirect.
- **Air service development** – a diversification/hedging strategy to increase the range of carriers and routes operated at the airport to reduce exposure to a particular carrier or market.
- **Development of non-aeronautical revenues and ancillary activities** - revenue diversification as a risk mitigation strategy. By relying less on aircraft operations and passenger enplanements, airports can reduce their systemic revenue uncertainty associated with the air travel industry.

The greater flexibility that real options provide can have significant value to a decision maker. However, real options sometimes (but not always) impose a cost. The trade-off between the real option's value and its cost will determine whether to go ahead with the option.

Framework and methodology

This section summarises the primary output from the Transport Research Board study, a methodological framework which aids airports in identifying and quantifying risk, developing mitigation strategies and evaluating those strategies.

The framework and related methodologies have been developed from research on forecasting techniques and flexible planning. It is based on a detailed review of the relevant literature and of currently used methodologies and common practices used to incorporate uncertainties into airport planning, and refined through application to a number of case studies. The systems analysis framework and the related methodologies are designed to assist airport decision makers with:

- Identifying and characterizing risks (threats or opportunities), including their plausibility and magnitude.
- Assessing the impact of these threats and opportunities, i.e., determining what can happen, to whom, and when.
- Developing response strategies to avoid or lessen the impact of threats, or to foster the realization of opportunities.

The framework is designed to be general enough to accommodate a variety of airports and projects, and scalable in order to match the methodology with the resources and needs of each airport. The framework allows planners to consider a broad range of events and risks, and helps them anticipate possible changes that might follow. It is not intended to replace the master planning process or any other planning or decision making model. Instead, the framework augments the master plan with methodologies which allow airport planners to analyse risk and uncertainty and incorporate relevant mitigation measures into the planning process.

The framework provides different options generating output with differing levels of detail and depth suitable for different airport sizes as well as different planning projects. The selection of the different methodology options is at the discretion of the user.

The systems analysis framework is comprised of five key steps. Each step can be executed at differing levels of quantitative detail depending on airport and project size, scope and complexity. The five key steps are as illustrated in Figure 2.3.

- Identify and quantify risk and uncertainty.
- Assess the cumulative impacts.
- Identify risk response strategies.
- Evaluate risk response strategies.
- Risk tracking and evaluation.

In the following section, the five steps will be discussed.

Figure 2.3. **Systems analysis framework**

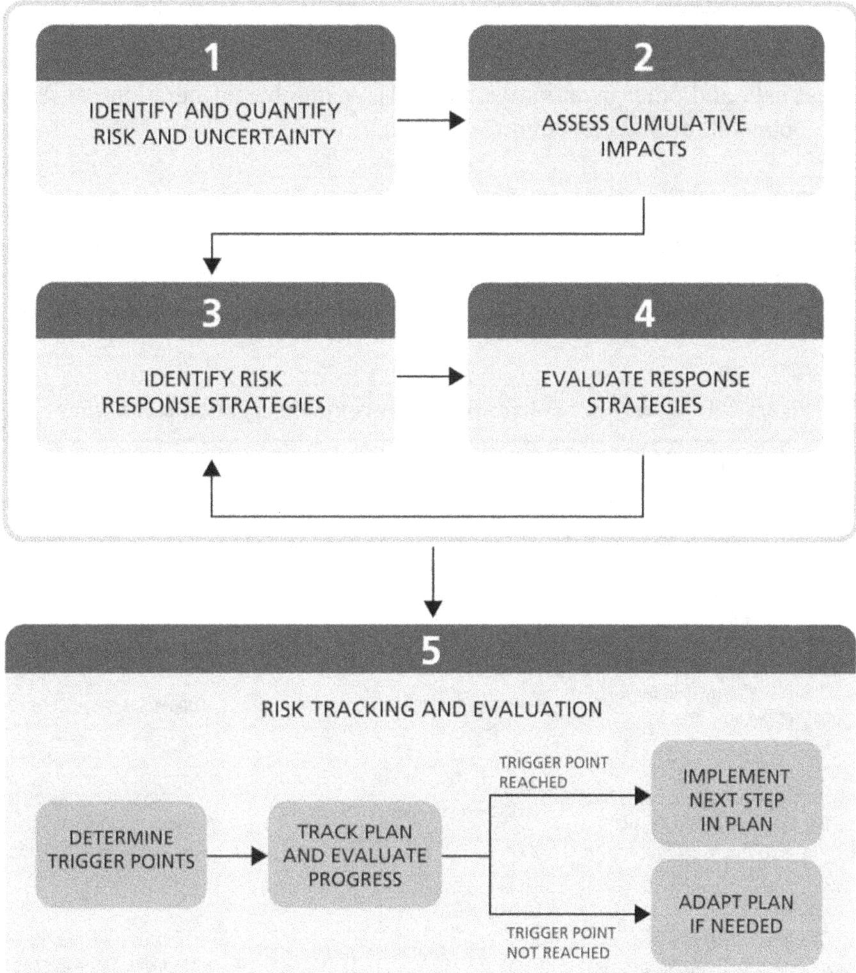

Source: ACRP Report 76, 2012.

Step 1: Identify and quantify risk and uncertainty

Using a combination of data-based and judgment-based methodologies, the first step identifies and attempts to quantify risks and uncertainties facing the airport. The ultimate output from this step is a Risk Register which summarises what is known about each risk and can feed this information into the other steps of the process. The guidebook identifies risk factors that have affected airports in the past and provides techniques to identify additional risks specific to the airport and to quantify their implications. In this paper, most approaches and tools to identify and quantify risks are just briefly discussed.

In order to identify and quantify the risks and uncertainty facing an airport, the following questions need to be answered for each possible risk factor:

- What is the particular risk/uncertainty?
- What is the probability or likelihood of that risk/uncertainty occurring?
- What will be the impact of the risk/uncertainty factor, should it occur, both in the short and long-term.

This information will be obtained from "brainstorming" and elicitation techniques, as well as from analysis of historical data and other quantitative methods. A number of iterations of the process may be required in order to obtain all of the relevant information.

Elicitation techniques

Eliciting information from airport management and other stakeholders can be a key element of the risk and uncertainty identification and quantification process. Figure 2.4 provides an overview of the methods available to airport planners to elicit probability and/or measures of impact, and to summarise elicited opinions.

Figure 2.4. **Overview of elicitation and group aggregation techniques**

Technique	Description	Pros	Cons
Delphi	Refinement of experts' opinions by providing feedback through a series of surveys, without open interactions.	Consensus may be reached relatively quickly.	No direct interactions between experts
Statistical groups	One-time survey of experts' opinions, without interactions.	Experts cannot influence each other.	Consensus may not be reached.
Nominal groups	Refinement of experts' opinions by a series of survey-based sessions, with interactions.	Consensus may be reached relatively quickly.	Discussions may be time-consuming; some experts may be influenced by others.
Unstructured interacting groups	One-time survey of experts' opinions, with interactions, possibly in a workshop setting.	Consensus may be reached through discussions.	Discussions may be time-consuming; some experts may be influenced by others.

As well as identifying risk factors, all of these methods can be used to elicit a subjective assessment of both the probability and the impact of different risk factors. Having obtained input on a range of risk factors, the information gathered can be represented in a simplified form, as illustrated in Figure 2.5. The summary plot diagram can effectively provide feedback to the participants and help identify critical uncertainties (those with high probabilities and/or high impacts).

Figure 2.5. **Illustrative example of a summary plot of identified risks and uncertainties**

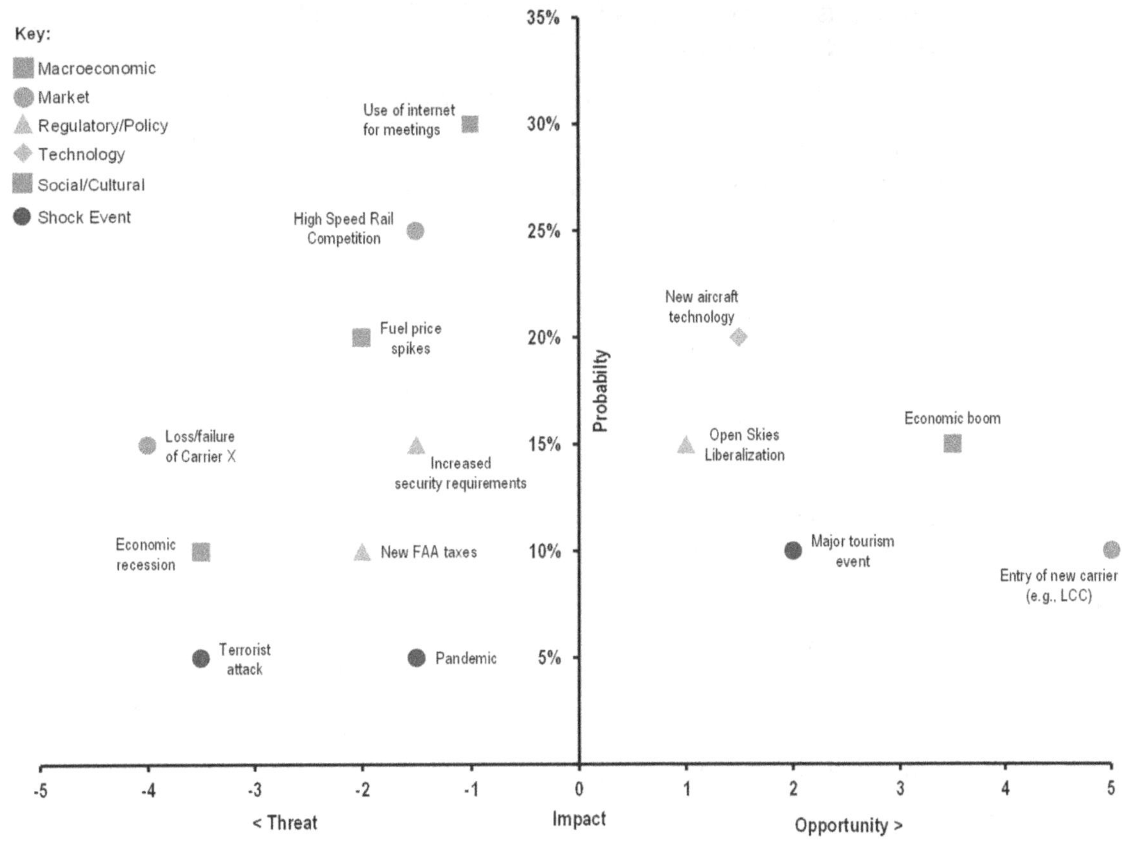

Source: ACRP Report 76, 2012.

Approaches to quantifying probabilities and impacts

In some cases, historical data can be used to determine the likelihood and probable impact of recurring events. In this context, recurring events refer to those events that have occurred at least once in the past, and may occur again in the future. They may be recurring within the aviation industry but not necessarily at a specific airport.

This approach, however, has some limitations. First - and this is a critique applicable to most forecasting techniques used in airport planning - the past is not necessarily a good indicator of what will happen in the future. Second, isolating the impact of a specific event on a measure of airport activity may not be straightforward due to data limitations (data may be limited in quantity, quality, or both) or inadequate statistical skills. Third, historical data is only marginally relevant to assess the likelihood of "rare events", or to quantify threats and opportunities whose frequency and/or impacts vary with no apparent pattern over time.

Planners choosing to evaluate the probable impact of future events based on historical data can use one of the following methods:

- Use evidence and "priors" published in the literature.
- Use an existing airport activity forecasting model, calibrated specifically for the airport being reviewed, and conduct sensitivity analysis and/or scenario testing.
- Perform statistical analysis of airport activity data, whereby the impact of a past event - or a series of past events - is estimated while accounting for the influence of other factors (i.e., holding everything else constant).

The level of analysis can be enhanced to provide greater detailed on the risk factors:

- **Direct and indirect impacts.** An important consideration in the quantification of impacts is the distinction between direct and indirect impacts. In a direct impact, the occurrence of an event directly affects the activity of the airport being analysed. Examples of events that create direct impacts include the destruction of airport infrastructure by a hurricane or the de-hubbing/downsizing of an airline at a specific airport, which directly affects the number of passengers that use that particular facility. On the other hand, an indirect impact is when the occurrence of an event indirectly affects the activity at the airport (usually through a well-established transmission mechanism). Examples of indirect impacts include a global economic recession or an increase in jet fuel prices. A recession will reduce employment, consumer confidence and disposable income ultimately weakening the demand for air travel. Likewise, increases in jet fuel costs can feed through into higher ticket prices, which dampen demand (or result in air service cutbacks by carriers). It may be necessary to undertake additional analysis to understand the impact of certain variables on traffic levels.
- **Probability distributions**. In some cases it may be possible to estimate distributions from historical data. For example, data could be collected on quarterly or annual GDP growth rates and a distribution fitted which approximates the distribution of data. Distribution fitting can be done with many statistical packages or with specific risk analysis software. An example of distribution fitting is shown in Figure 2.6. The histogram bars are the observed historical distribution of GDP growth rates, and the black line is the statistical distribution fitted to the histogram.

Figure 2.6. **Example of distribution fitting (using illustrative data)**

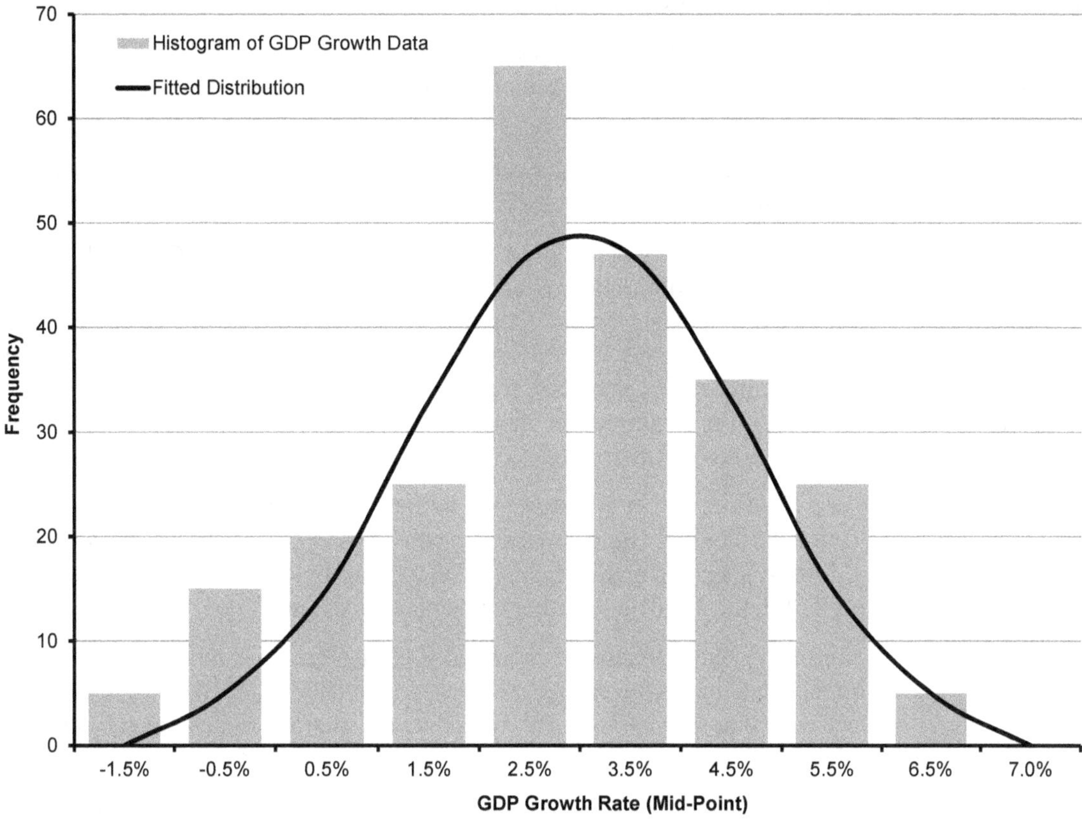

Source: ACRP Report 76, 2012.

- **Correlations and dependencies**. All risks and uncertainties are not necessary independent of each other. The occurrence of one event may increase or decrease the probability of another event occurring. For example, high fuel prices can increase the likelihood of an economic recession, or the entry of an aggressive low cost carrier can increase the likelihood of an incumbent carrier exiting, etc. Furthermore, there can also be dependencies over time, such that the probability of an event depends on whether it has occurred before. Such dependencies can be captured by specifying correlation coefficients between variations. However, in practice this can be difficult to communicate in the elicitation process and can greatly increase the complexity of the analysis.

Step 2: Assess cumulative impacts

This step involves analysis and modelling to assess the combined impact of the identified risks and the implications for traffic development. It can encompass the development of a structural model incorporating uncertainty whose primary purpose is to evaluate the combined effect of multiple risks on airport activity and help define and assess alternative courses of action (response strategies).

The first undertaking consists of developing an analysis of the risks identified in the previous step, paying attention to the way the relationships between events, variables and outcomes will be modeled, as well as the "transmission mechanisms" between them. The goal is to create a model that captures – with as much precision as possible – the impacts uncertain events will have on relevant indicators of airport activity.

The model can range from a simple trend model based on assumed growth rates, to a complex multivariate model of the airport. It is anticipated that most airports will fall into one of two camps:

- Airport planners have access to a calibrated activity forecasting model (e.g., multivariate regression model of demand, simulation model, etc.), which can be used for uncertainty analysis and scenario testing.
- Airport planners do not have a forecasting model, instead relying on outside forecasts (e.g., the FAA Terminal Area Forecast).

In the first case, the existing model can be used as the basis for the assessment of cumulative impacts. For example, the model may contain parameters related to economic activity which can be used to assess the impact of macroeconomic risk factors. The model has the benefit that it already contains information on the "transmission mechanisms" by which chance events and other sources of uncertainty affect relevant variables and outcomes. Nevertheless, modifications may be necessary to allow for risk factors not addressed in the model. For example, the model may not contain any parameters specifically related to shock events (pandemics, terrorism attacks, etc.).

In the case where there is no access to a forecasting model but the airport does have an outside forecast, the cumulative impacts can still be assessed by considering the likely deviation from the forecast. For example, the loss of a carrier might cause traffic to drop below the forecast level and then gradually recover some or all of the lost traffic (as other carriers enter the market).

Once a model for quantifying the impacts of uncertainty is in place, the next activity consists of quantifying cumulative impacts of uncertain events on airport activity. To do this, it is necessary to define the different risk scenarios that will be analysed as well as the characteristics of each one of them. Tools such as scenario analysis and Monte Carlo simulation are commonly used at this stage.

The scenario analysis is a less technically demanding approach which is suitable for smaller airport and smaller sized planning projects while Monte Carlo is more technically demanding but provides a richer output and may be suitable for bigger airports and bigger scale projects. Again, the approach selected is at the discretion of the user.

The scenario analysis is described in more detail in the ACRP report. In this paper, we will provide a quick overview of the Monte Carlo simulation.

Monte Carlo simulations

Monte Carlo involves running the forecast model multiple times (generally thousands of times), each time with the inputs (and in many cases, the parameters) being randomly generated based on the probability distribution assumed for each input (or parameter). Under this approach, each forecast produced is associated with a probability of occurrence based on the individual probabilities of occurrence associated with the variables within the model. The probabilities associated with each outcome allow more quantitative analysis to be undertaken, providing airport planners with a richer set of information.

Figure 2.7 illustrates a simple example of the use of the Monte Carlo simulation approach to analyse the impact of risk and uncertainty on future traffic operations at an airport. The total number of aircraft operations at an airport – identified by F – is modelled as a function of airport taxes, average load factor and average aircraft capacity. However, it is also assumed that these three variables, along with the price-elasticity of demand for air travellers (i.e., the elasticity of demand for that specific airport by passengers with respect to airport taxes) have uncertain behaviour with well-defined probability density functions. Through the use of Monte Carlo simulations several point estimates for the total number of aircraft operations are calculated based on individual "draws" from each probability distribution function associated with each. At the end of the simulation, all point estimates for aircraft operations obtained through this process can be used to construct a probability distribution function for this output.

Figure 2.7. **An illustration of the use of Monte Carlo simulation techniques to account for multiple sources of uncertainty**

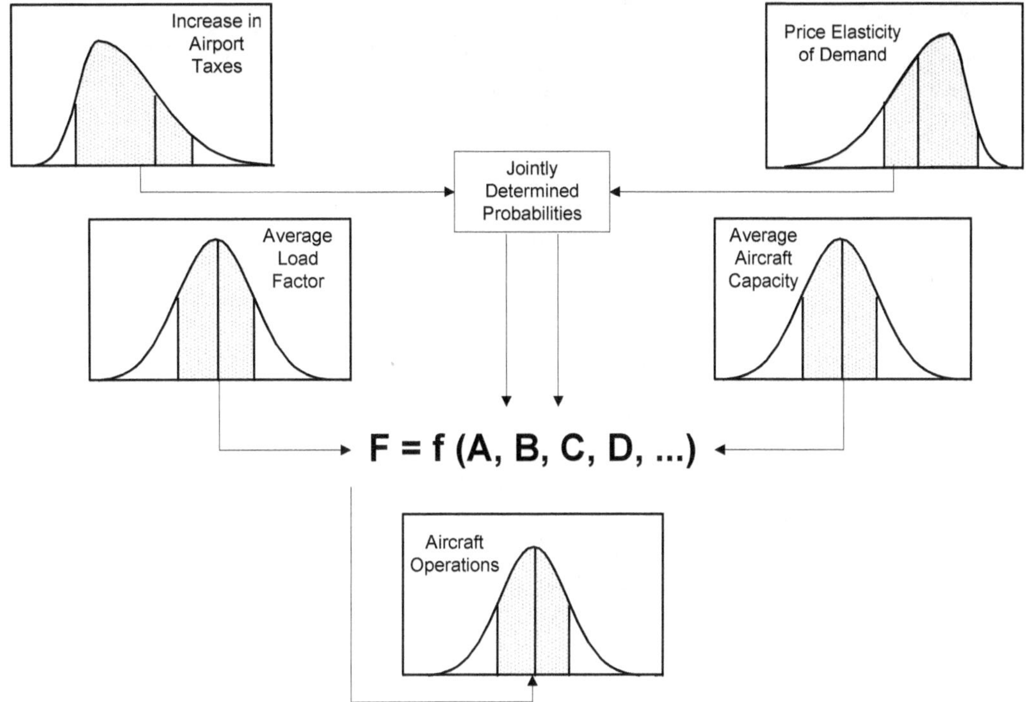

Source: ACRP Report 76, 2012.

Monte Carlo simulation can handle both direct and indirect impacts, both of which can be modeled with considerable complexity. Monte Carlo simulation can also be used to address concerns about statistical or model error. For example, the impact of a changing relationship between traffic growth and GDP growth can be explored by randomizing the GDP parameter within the model.

The Monte Carlo method can be very powerful – large numbers of uncertainties can be considered simultaneously, each of which can have various different, randomised characteristics. Interactions or correlations between the variables can also be modelled as well as various different timings of events. Given the complexity, and the need for repeated random sampling of inputs or variables, Monte Carlo is performed by a computer. There are a number of software products which can be used to conduct Monte Carlo simulation.

The output from the Monte Carlo simulations can be presented in a number of ways. The histogram in Figure 2.8 provides information on the probability density – or probability of occurrence. For example, the chart indicates that, when all risks and sources of uncertainty being considered simultaneously, there is an 80% probability that the number of enplanements at the airport will be 2.2 million or less in Year 10 (or a 20% probability that traffic will exceed 2.2 million in Year 10).

So-called Tornado diagrams can also be derived from the Monte Carlo output, which help identify critical risk factors. Time series plot of the mostly likely or base forecast along with the "prediction interval" produced from Monte Carlo is another option to present the outcome of a Monte Carlo simulation. Examples of these are provided in Figures 2.9 and 2.10.

Figure 2.8. **Illustrative probability density and cumulative probability output from the Monte Carlo simulations**

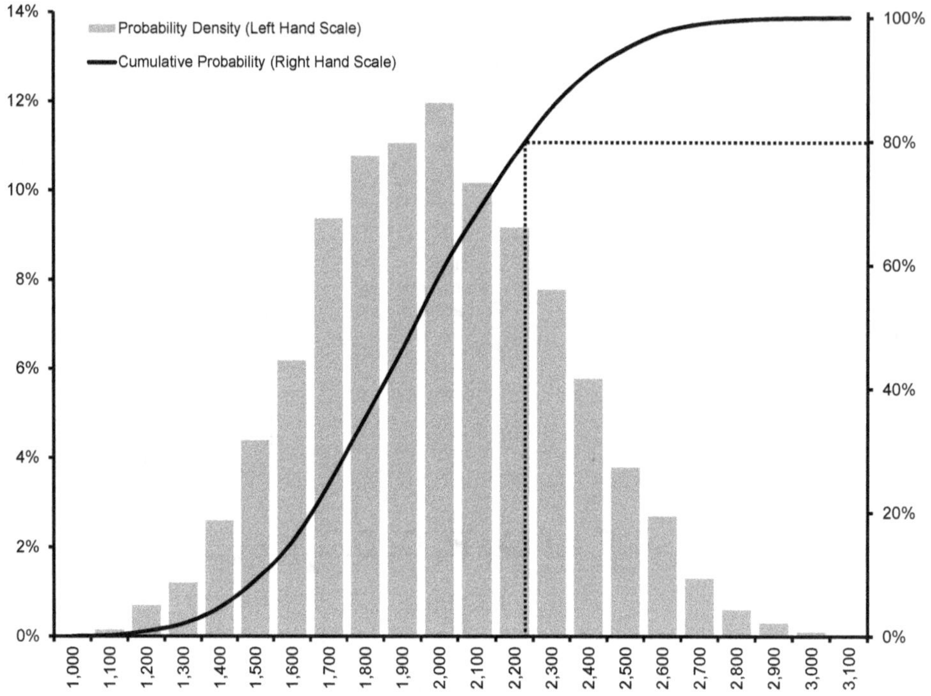

Source: ACRP Report 76, 2012.

Figure 2.9. **Illustrative Tornado diagram**

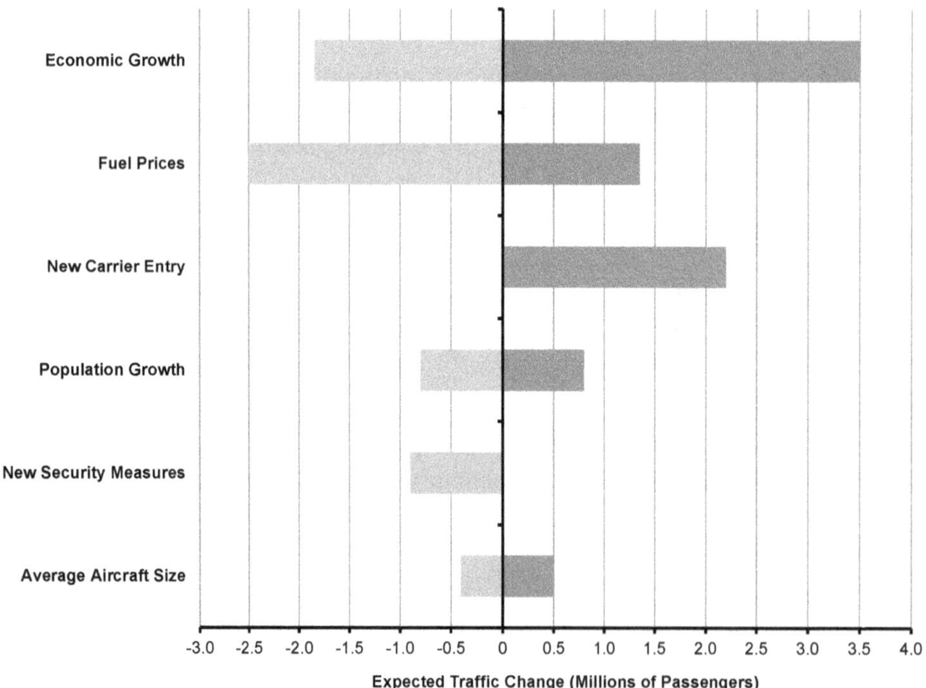

Source: ACRP Report 76, 2012.

Figure 2.10. **Illustrative prediction intervals**

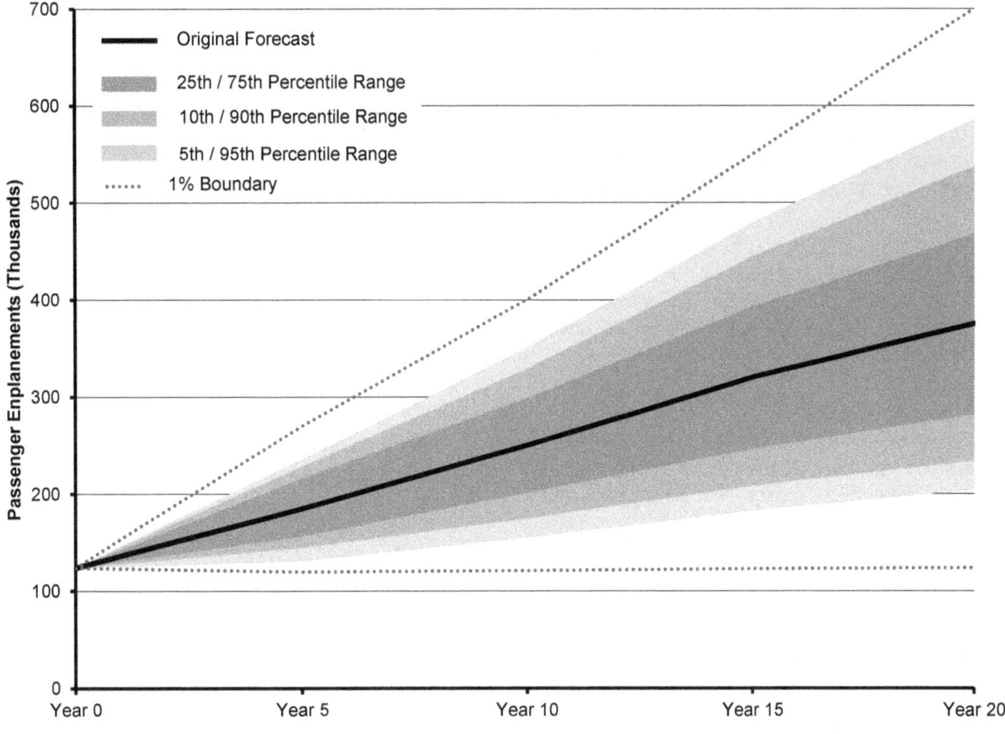

Source: ACRP Report 76, 2012.

With the Monte Carlo analysis in particular, there may be a temptation to ignore or pay little attention to the extreme outcomes produced by the analysis (i.e., the far tails of the output distribution). After all, the model output itself indicates a very low probability of such an outcome. However, many of the unexpected events that have occurred to airports would likely have been assessed low probability before the event occurred. Obviously basing the airport planning entirely on such extreme outcomes is not desirable. However, there may be value in examining these extreme outcomes and considering whether the airport plan is robust to such extremes (or can be made robust).

Step 3: Identify risk response strategies

Based on the output from Steps 1 and 2, this step identifies risk response strategies that will help avoid or mitigate negative risks and exploit or enhance positive risks. It is often the case that the same strategies can address a broad range of risks. One key finding from this research is that many risk strategies were applicable regardless of the risk profile or even the circumstances of the airport.

The risk and uncertainties facing airports present both threats and opportunities. As set out in Table 2.1, there are four broad categories of response to these threats and opportunities.

Table 2.1. **General risk response strategies to threats and opportunities**

Threats	Opportunities
Avoid Action is taken to eliminate the impact of a risk. Some threats can be avoided entirely by changing operations or eliminating practices deemed "risky." This will often incur a cost. Eliminating risky practices might disappoint stakeholders or degrade the overall business case.	Exploit Make a proactive decision to take action and show that an opportunity is realised.
Transfer The impact of the risk is transferred to another party, willing to and better able to handle the risk (such as an insurance company or investors in a futures market). This typically involves payment of a fee (e.g., outsourcing to a skilled expert) or a premium (e.g., insurance).	Share Assign ownership of the opportunity to a third-party who is best able to capture the benefit for the operation. Examples include forming risk-sharing partnerships, teams, or joint ventures, which can be established with the express purpose of managing opportunities.
Mitigate Action is taken to lessen the expected impact of a risk. Mitigation generally requires positive actions, and can have a resource cost. These actions should be considered new practices and controlled like any other airport operations. They may affect the airport operating budget, but are often preferable to a "do-nothing" approach (see discussion on evaluation in the next section).	Enhance Take action to increase the probability and/or impact of the opportunity for the benefit of the operation. Seek to facilitate or strengthen the cause of the opportunity, and proactively target and reinforce the conditions under which it may occur.
Accept No action is taken. After trying to avoid, transfer, or mitigate the threats, the operation will be left with residual risks - threats that cannot be reduced further. In active acceptance, airport management may set up a "contingency reserve fund" to account for the residual expected value of the remaining risks. A passive form of acceptance simply acknowledges the risk and moves forward with existing practices without reserves, which may seem sensible for risks with small expected values.	Accept Take no action when a response may be too costly to be effective, or when the risk is uncontrollable and no practical action may be taken to specifically address it.

The general approach to developing a set of response strategies corresponding to a predefined risk profile is similar to that of risk identification. There is no standalone method or tool that can offer the "correct" set of strategies, given the nature of the risks being analysed. Furthermore, given the diversity of airport activity risks, the set of recommended strategies should be flexible and scalable enough to be implemented by airports of different sizes and locations.

One approach is to review the most current aviation practices. By reviewing practices at other airports, planners can understand how to develop and implement response strategies. This approach can also be used to assess the pros and cons of various strategies and areas for improvement, based on their performance in the past.

The development of a risk response strategy can also involve elicitation from stakeholders and subject matter experts. For example, a workshop can be held after the risks and uncertainties have been identified and quantified. The purpose of the workshop is to elicit recommendations and consensus on response strategies that are feasible and likely to align with the airport's overall strategic plans. Workshop participants can engage in develop response strategies using the same aggregation techniques as those identified for risk quantification.

A similar approach is *scenario planning,* where participants are presented with various forecast outcomes and asked to devise response strategies to address these outcomes. This approach provides a realistic and plausible future scenario (or set of scenarios) upon which the response strategies can be based, rather than an abstract list of risk factors. A possible shortcoming, however, is that the scenarios being analysed (and for which a response strategy has been formulated) may be different from actual, future conditions. Therefore, the participants should be encouraged to adopt a *real options* approach, i.e., selecting risk response strategies that provide the maximum amount of flexibility for the airport. The response strategies should avoid committing to long-term courses of action since this creates inflexibilities that are costly to correct in case changes need to be made in the near to mid future.

The ACRP report developed by Inter*VISTAS* sets out a range of airport-specific strategies and approaches and provides guidance on the type of risks they address (including those described previously titled *Methods for better addressing uncertainty in forecasting and planning*).

Step 4: Evaluate risk response strategies

Step 4 undertakes a qualitative and quantitative evaluation of the risk response strategies identified in Step 3 to demonstrate their effectiveness and value for money. This may result in revisions to the risk response strategies. The risk response strategies from Step 3 are designed to reduce the likelihood or impact of potential threats and to capitalise on possible opportunities. Inevitably, the choice of a strategy to respond to a particular risk is difficult; in particular, because its effectiveness cannot be fully understood until the risk actually occurs. An evaluation of the economic and/or financial value of risk response strategies can be conducted to assist in the selection. The evaluation serves a number of purposes: identify the highest value risk response strategy, demonstrate robustness over a wide range of outcomes, and determine value for money.

In order to perform a detailed evaluation of the risk responses, it is necessary to perform an appraisal of a response strategy under different circumstances, ranging from the traditional evaluation using the "best estimate" for the effectiveness of the response strategy to situations where the effectiveness is given extreme values (i.e., conducting a stress test). The evaluation process relies on the comparison between the degree of usefulness of a risk response strategy – in terms of its effectiveness to alter the probability of occurrence of a risk or its impact on airport activity – and its implementation cost. In more advanced analysis, the benefits of implementing a risk reduction strategy can be monetised and compared to the monetary cost associated with the implementation of the strategy.

The approaches for evaluating the risk response strategies can range from largely qualitative - relying primarily on judgment and expert opinion – to principally quantitative.

The largely qualitative approach involves assessing the risk response strategy (or strategies) against a number of traffic scenarios, and evaluating them based on judgment, historical examples, and simple quantification.

An example is the qualitative approach that was taken to determine the need for a second airport in Sydney, Australia. During the 1980s, the Australian government grappled with the issue of whether a second airport would be required for the city of Sydney. The analysis focused on whether land should be reserved which would allow a second airport to be built in the future. This decision was considered under three different traffic growth scenarios. This evaluation was based on reasoned judgment and did not require complex analysis. It showed that acquiring a site generally provided the best outcome across the scenarios and, as a result, the government of Australia did acquire a site for the second airport. This approach can be applied to a single response strategy or can be used to consider a number of strategies in combination.

Figure 2.12 shows the Sydney example as a decision tree. The nodes of the tree represent decision points or event outcomes. The advantage of using Decision Trees is that it can handle a great combination of response strategies. However, a complex system could involve large numbers of decision points and events, resulting in a very large, and potentially unmanageable decision tree (computer software is available to make this process more manageable).

Figure 2.11. **Decision tree for second Sydney airport**

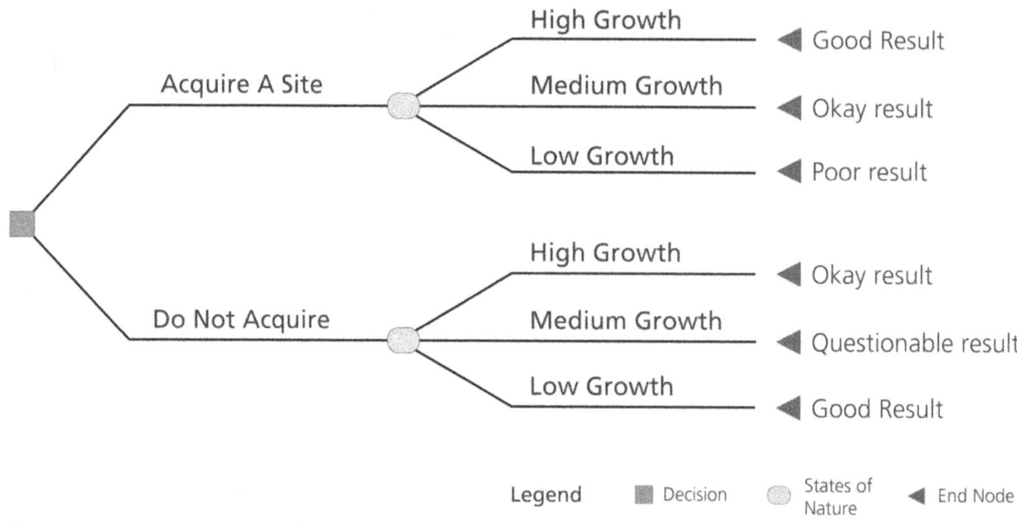

Source: ACRP Report 76, 2012.

A more quantitative approach is to use the result of Monte Carlo simulation of the traffic forecasts. Monte Carlo simulations provide a rich source of information to be used in the quantitative evaluation of risk response strategies. Typically, thousands of forecasts are generated by the Monte Carlo simulation, each with a probability attached. This allows for a variety of risk-based analytical procedures, including expected values. To calculate expected values, a measure of value must be selected and calculated which represents the desired outcome of the risk response strategies. The value could be capital costs, if the airport planner is looking for risk response strategies that minimise capital spending. Another measure used is Net Present Value (NPV) or the Expected Net Present Value (ENPV); both concepts (and related measures) are discussed in further detail in the ACRP report.

Step 5: Risk tracking and evaluation

This final step is slightly different to the others as it represents an on-going process of review and revision. Step 5 involves tracking risks and traffic over time and flagging potential issues, taking action prescribed in the risk response strategies if potential risks do materialise, and making updates and revisions to the airport risk profile and risk response strategies. The ultimate aim of Step 5's risk tracking and evaluation is to foster a high level of risk awareness and responsiveness within the organization.

Various tools and techniques can be used to aid in the tracking and evaluation of risk and uncertainty. Their selection will depend on the resources and time available and include:

- Tracking trigger points - identifying traffic level or other measures that would trigger certain actions or developments. Where a trigger point has been met or exceeded, the first task is to evaluate traffic levels to determine whether it is reasonably permanent and likely to be sustained in the future. Once there is a reasonable consensus that the trigger point has been met, the action or capital development specified can be initiated. As noted previously, downside (or defensive) trigger points can also be established which lead to project slowdowns or pauses.
- Establish a *risk management team* - Large airports in particular might choose to establish a Risk Management Team, comprised of airport personnel from different departments, whose activities have a direct connection to the identified risk factors (e.g., operations for infrastructure risks, marketing for airline related risk, etc.). The purpose of such a team is to

bring together various parts of the organization – marketing, planning, finance, operations, security, etc. – with each providing a unique perspective on the risk and uncertainties facing the airport.

- Periodic updates - Periodic (e.g., quarterly) update memos can serve as a communication tool to summarise the key risks, mitigation status, and changes to the risk profile. This memo can be developed by the Risk Management Team, if one has been established, or by an assigned member of staff. The memo should incorporate a brief description of the current performance of the airport, any changes to the risk or traffic outlook, as well as a summary of what has changed since the previous analysis was completed.
- Annual review - Approximately once a year a review should be undertaken to "step back" and re-evaluate the airport's risks and the risk response strategies.
- Benchmarking - Seeking information from outside of the airport, to examine situations at other airports nationally and around the world. Events and activities at other airports may provide indicators of risks that could spread to the decision maker's own airport. In addition, the responses of these airports may provide information on which actions to take and which to avoid.

Conclusions

Differences between assumed and actual events significantly diminish the accuracy of airport activity forecasts developed with traditional techniques. A challenge in forecasting is dealing with the risks and uncertainties that drive a wedge between assumed and actual outcomes.

While it can be instructive to explore singly the effect on airport activity forecasts of assumptions made about this or that particular outcome, in the real world literally every important outcome will differ from the one initially assumed. In reality, forecasts must consider the cumulative and simultaneous effect of risk and uncertainty in every factor important to the airport activity forecasts. Therefore, this research developed a unified systems analysis framework that enables airport activity forecasters to identify risk factors, to understand the extent to which each risk factor introduces uncertainty into activity forecasts, and to ascertain how the risks and uncertainties are likely to interact so as to examine realistically their combined implications for air traffic going forward.

Although a methodology framework has been developed, it need not, and should not, be viewed as a "one-size fits all" approach to all airports and all projects. Airport planners can apply the systems analysis methodology at different levels of quantitative and qualitative detail ranging from almost no quantitative analysis at all to highly sophisticated statistical and simulation based methods. In all cases, however, there is a very important role for management and stakeholder discussion and consensus and "elicitation methods" are presented as part of the systems analysis methodology.

In applying the developed methodology, airport forecasting and planning will be more robust to uncertainty and risk. However, there is still work to be done to improve the robustness of airport forecasting and planning.

In particular, there is a need to address political risk, which can alter the appropriate design, timing or financial arrangements for airport development. While political risks can be less amenable to quantitative treatment than economic, demographic and other statistically measurable variables, they can be no less significant in their implications for airport plans. For example, as the case of London illustrates, runway development is often a source of significant political risk and systematic approaches to explicitly dealing with such risk would be productive. Infrastructure is in general susceptible to political factors. Further research is required to more fully and formally integrate political risk into the systems analysis methodology.

References

For further description of the debate around Sydney airport, see Expanding Airport Capacity under Constraints in Large Urban Areas, D. Thompson, S. Perkins and K. van Dender, OECD Discussion Paper No. 2013-24, December 2013.

De Neufville, R. and J. Barber, "Deregulation induced volatility of airport traffic." Transportation Planning and Technology, 16(2) (1991) pp. 117-128.

Addressing Uncertainty About Future Airport Activity Levels in Airport Decision Making, ACRP Report 76, 2012. Lambert-St. Louis International Airport Passenger Statistics, and FAA Terminal Area Forecast, 1998-2015.

Chapter 3. Choice models and contemporary airport demand forecasting

Benedikt Mandel[1]

During the last two decades, as the air transport industry has changed rapidly, traditional data sources have struggled to keep up and continue to reflect the true state of the industry. This paper describes an alternative way of forecasting air transport demand that addresses these data issues and presents alternative data sources. It explains the econometric system approach developed by MKmetric which includes a new mathematical framework that reflects the consumers' decision process and overcomes some of the shortfalls of traditional models.

The system approach developed is based on the classical 4 step procedure, namely generation, distribution, modal split and assignment. However it models the interdependent choices such as modal choice, airport and route choice, access and egress simultaneously. The model mirrors consumer behaviour using logistic functions whereby the mathematical form is flexible so that thresholds can be included. The elasticities of consumers to characteristics of the alternatives (e.g. time, cost, frequency, alliance) allow measurement of demand effects from changes in the transport system, e.g. services, infrastructure.

The approach uses dynamic, rather than fixed, airport catchment areas. These are a function of the attractiveness of the alternative transport opportunities available for each trip. Demand forecasts for an airport or a route consider the competitors endogenously. In addition, new methods are proposed to compute network impedance, which reflects the attractiveness of each alternative based on the infrastructure networks of all modes. The full potential of this approach is demonstrated by some examples.

1. MKmetric GmbH, Karlsruhe, Germany.

I am grateful to Oliver Schnell for his contributions to the application chapter and his comments on drafts of the paper. The approach outlined builds on a variety of research projects partially supported by the European Commission and the German Federal Ministry of Transport and Digital Infrastructure in combination with airports and airlines. The responsibility for any remaining shortcomings remains the author's.

Introduction

Demand forecasting is a useful tool that can provide a variety of stakeholders - airport and airline owners, potential investors and the government - with useful insight into the potential future developments relating to both airports and airlines. For example, the government may want to know the effects of taxation, air service agreements or the necessity of infrastructure investments for upgrading an existing airport or building a new airport. Regional authorities, when airport owners, may want to analyse an airport's potential to attract passengers or measure the potential impact of PSOs (public service obligations) on regional connectivity. Airports may want to shed light on how their portfolio of destinations may develop and airlines may want to look into potential rearrangements of their route network.

These questions cannot be answered without looking into demand forecasts. Route development, airline marketing, infrastructure investment, competition analysis, risk assessment, policy development or tactical and strategic simulations of scenarios cannot be credibly conducted without building on demand forecasts.

The value of the approach presented in this paper is that it can provide the stakeholders with demand forecasts under changing conditions in the market for aviation. The approach allows for conducting long term forecasts as well as short term simulations that focus on the immediate effects of changing consumer behaviour. The short term simulations are thus particularly valuable to short term planning by airports and airlines.

Forecasting in a rapidly changing market for aviation

For decades, aviation demand models have been based on historic data (statistics) and full market samples (BSP[1], MIDT[2]). These data sets are predominantly used for traffic forecasts at a particular airport location. For route network analysis, most forecasts rely on globally standardised data sets, such as the OAG Schedules Data that combines flight schedules of over 900 airlines.[3]

Since the 1990's, the airline business models have rapidly evolved due to different global factors, notably liberalisation, deregulation and globalisation. Liberal air service agreement policy tore down barriers, opened new markets and increased competition. In consequence, the market was entered by many new players, including low cost carriers. Meanwhile, in Europe, military airport conversions for civilian use and upgrading of existing regional airports have enriched the airport choices for consumers. Finally, the emergence of the Gulf and Turkish carriers and their respective hubs has redefined the structure of the long haul network, especially between Europe and points East and South. This lead to a necessary wave of consolidation in Europe and the US as incumbent carriers positioned themselves against new entrants and, as a result, the rise of global airline alliances and strategic joint ventures to defend markets, leverage synergies and influence consumer behaviour, through customer loyalty programmes. In the meantime, airlines bought new types of aircraft, such as the new Airbus A350 and Boeing 787 Dreamliner, which could allow for significant fuel savings and more flexible operations. Also new products on board have been developed and a higher differentiation in the fare structure with tariff decomposition driven by aggressive yield management came up, especially for connecting flights. All these factors contributed to the creation of more dynamic and responsive route networks, as carriers, particularly low cost, can adopt a trial and error approach to route development.

Low cost carriers were particularly successful in Europe, where the single market in the EU which enabled the rise of low cost carriers throughout the Union, combined with the Schengen treaty abolishing customs control within the EU, has encouraged consumers to undertake short, get-away trips. Migration has also created opportunities for increased travel to visit friends and relatives as air transport continues to become more affordable.

Last but not least the consumer has been educated to be more sensitive to price the opportunities presented by the unbundling of services. Through web-based IT-systems, passengers can now customise their entire air travel experience. Meanwhile, in an effort to drive down prices, airlines have increased direct sales channels, relying less and less on global distribution system (GDS) and the cost these incur.

In conclusion, the radical transformation of the air transport industry requires a re-evaluation of the appropriateness of classical forecasting approaches that are based on trends of the past or service of quality prolongations (Quality of Service Indicators or QSI). These approaches fail to reflect the radical market development and are less reliant than in the past due to an increasing share of direct ticket sales.

One way of dealing with the challenges outlined in this paper is to develop a forecast that would be based on modelling the consumer behaviour , which starts from modelling the true origin and destination of the passenger rather than their airport of origin and destination. Therefore the modeller's point of view has to turn from the airport to the region as the starting point of the trip decision so that the traditional static view becomes a consumer-oriented dynamic one. Thus airport catchments are no longer defined by fixed isochrones to determine the airport's passenger potential; they are flexible reflecting the competitive situation on a route by route basis.

Model capabilities

The challenges outlined above require a demand forecast model capable of properly adapting to a changing marketplace and the diminishing quality of traditional aviation data. When forecasting the effects of future market changes these need to be measured, or considered, within a consistent modelling approach. Thus, irrespective of which approach is used, the following features need to be reflected in the model:

- **Competition of destinations, e.g. complementary or substitution:**

  Regions are competing with each other for inbound tourism and investments to increase employment and social welfare more generally. Thus the air connectivity of a region is an important asset for its development perspectives. Increased consumer choice in parallel with decreasing costs encourages consumers to undertake additional trips.

- **Modal competition:**

  Surface networks offer alternative travel options in short haul markets which can compete with air services due to attractive travel times and prices, especially high speed rail.

- **Modal co-operation:**

  The extension of surface networks can provide for more intensive co-operation between modes as well. Beside the classical highway access, airport railway stations on a high speed rail network most effectively increase the catchment area of an airport, substituting feeder flights and facilitating rail & fly services for medium and long haul travel.

- **Intra-modal competition:**

  A high density of airports with overlapping destination portfolios from different type of carriers usually enhances competition between carriers. The degree of competition depends on the way in which those airports are embedded in the surface transport networks, their service offer in terms of airline providers, and other characteristics, such as time, price, frequency, operation days, slots capacity, that are relevant to the passenger choice.

- **Interdependency of the different decision levels of the consumers**, e.g. slot choice, airport choice, access/egress choice, mode choice and travel demand:

  As a trip does not start at the airport, the whole travel chain should be considered, starting from access/egress of airports, the time of day the trip takes place, the route taken, as well as the door-to-door time and cost of travel.

- **Consumer preferences:**

  Different types of consumers show different preferences to product characteristics; some seek flexible and frequent services while others value lower fares. The consumers might be captive to product types and inelastic to pricing if frequent service is their preferred feature for example. Models need to reflect utility to consumers by consumer, embedding the characteristics of travel alternatives (e.g. time, cost, frequency, operation days, alliance or online connection) in their functional form.

- **Network effects:**

  Due to a rapid rise of the hub-and-spoke airline business models, consumers can now choose to fly point to point or indirectly, often through large global hubs. This development necessitates thinking in terms of entire networks to cover local and global effects in parallel. Consumers with a low value of time accept significant detours in exchange for lower air fares. Moreover, consumers who belong to airline loyalty programmes often choose longer indirect routes in order to reap the benefits of these programmes. Without considering the route network dynamics, it is thus difficult to determine the market attractiveness of an airport.

Furthermore, airlines and airports must also consider the policy environment in which they operate and the available technology. Considering the factors outlined above can allow for analysing the complex picture of passenger choice (see Figure 3.1).

Figure 3.1. **Consumers' complex alternative travel opportunities**

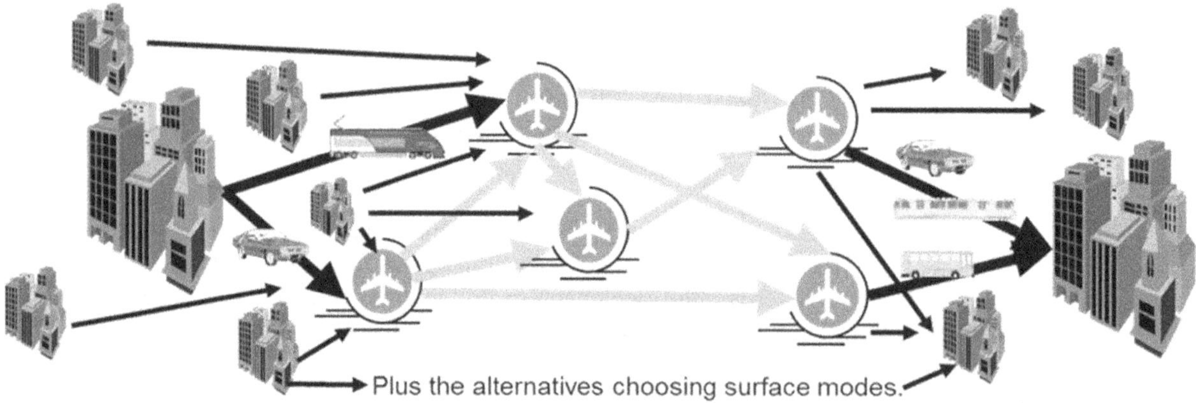

To satisfy all criteria mentioned above a consistent system approach with various econometric models dealing with the different requirements, implications and dynamic networks needs to be used in order to account for various interdependencies. .

Data implications

Both the MIDT and BSP databases, which had been the workhorse of understanding demand and routing, no longer cover all necessary data aspects, due to the emergence of direct sales and the exclusion from their data of low cost carriers (LCC) and charter carriers. IATA acknowledges this and in consequence products like PaxIS are no longer as accurate for airports and airlines (IATA World Passenger Symposium Singapore 2011). At the Symposium it was stated by Bryan Wilson[4] that PaxIS has lost 35% of total data (70% in Europe) and that it is no longer useful for many clients. IATA has, however, developed techniques to make reliable forecasts on the sample of data still available.

In parallel to the shrinking data sample the Global Distribution Systems (GDS) like Abacus, Amadeus, Galileo, Infinity, Sabre, Travelport, Travelsky, Worldspan etc. are fighting to defend the dominance of their Marketing Information Data Tape (MIDT), there ongoing legal challenges over the use of the BSP data. GDS providers want to protect and invent own products with customised solutions. In 2011 IATA reacted to the insufficient data situation by offering an alternative product, the Direct Data Service[5] (DDS). IATA invites travel agencies, airlines, and airports to share data on different granularity levels by signing a Contribution and License Data Agreement (CLDA). The CLDA stipulates that only the ones who signed in have access to the collected data.. But given the increased competitive situation and the strong engagement of carriers into direct sales techniques, why should airlines and airports provide these data to IATA-DDS so that competitors gain knowledge about markets to explore? Airlines already hardly share all market respective sales data within an alliance.

The use of direct sales is believed to diversified and further intensified. An IT trends survey[6] by SITA covering the world's 200 largest airlines in 2013 indicates that by 2016 the value of GDS ticket sales will decrease from 46% to 33% of the turnover of classic travel agents, while direct sales by airlines will increase from 54% to 67% of all tickets sold. Also, 63% of airlines will offer on-line services to change reservations, creating a wider gap between booking data and ticket data.

These survey results are confirmed by airline managers like Lionel Guérin[7], Chairman and CEO of HOP (Brit Air, Regional and Airlinair). He stated in an interview on 29 January 2013 "The other main new trend concerns the explosion of online sales: over 60% of Europeans systematically buy their airline tickets on the internet."

Direct sales are more cost effective for airlines, and can also render data that allows a more personalised service and facilitate upselling. The SITA study concludes that the sales of additional services will become much more important as airlines generate nearly nine times higher margins when selling the tickets to customers directly. Examination of the annual reports of the LCCs supports this argument. In consequence, the airlines are forced to intensify their direct sales efforts due to the multiple beneficial effects and the competitive advantage they can materialise. Due to globalisation and the strong competition airlines in all areas of the world diversify their business model as a logical step forward. As side effect the airlines reduce their dependence on distributors and save related costs when increasing mobile sales and other direct sale services.

Thus the existing data gaps with the traditional commercial data sources (BSP / MIDT), and the new products offered by IATA and the GDS provider, are likely to become greater with time. Often just the indirect sales are available and these are likely to represent a decreasing share of total sales, and at the same time LCC and Charter data is missing. The above mentioned data providers will have to depend on gap-handling procedures that can be seen to reduce the reliability of forecasts. In addition to these data problems, classical forecasting tools have to simultaneously tackle consumer- and market changes. This concerns not only the long-term investigations, also the classical Service of Quality Index (SQI) approaches struggle with a rapidly declining base of information.

Other data sources are needed to compensate for the shortfalls and to meet the requirements for forecasting models. MIDT or BSP data are not sufficient, neither in coverage and quality nor in dealing with the outlined challenges. Better forecasts can be achieved using public and mostly free data sources[8], below the main data types enabling an improved forecasting model are listed:

- Volume observations to cover the whole transport market, e.g.:
  - detailed Eurostat and national statistics (on flight, on stage)
  - publications of airports and airlines, IATA samples
  - publications of airport and airline associations
  - vehicle counts for road links
  - transport figures for rail.
- Consumer elasticity to identify the consumers' sensitivity, e.g.:
  - air transport passenger surveys at airports across Europe[9]
  - mobility and travel surveys across Europe
  - panel data of households.
- Mode networks to mirror the consumers' choice set, e.g.:
  - air schedules (OAG, Cedion, Innovata, ...)[10]
  - air traffic management data (EUROCONTROL, national representation)
  - information from the air transport industry (destination portfolios, load factors, …)
  - surface networks (road, bus)
  - railway, ferry schedules.
- Regional indicators to diversify regional attractiveness, e.g.:
  - socio-economic (UN, IWF, OECD, EZB, Eurostat, ...) partly
  - satellite data (Corine aggregates, ...)
  - tourist information
  - land use data
  - meteorological data.

These data allow building up, validating and running a forecasting model. The methodology to be applied is explained in the following section, where the basics of the econometric part are outlined. (For details refer to publications available on the web site www.mkm.de.)

The MKmetric model

This section describes the principle method and models used by MKmetric to forecast transport demand. The basic mathematical form of the models is shown with references for further reading and proofs. The description provides the essential characteristics and features required for a model to successfully to tackle the challenges outlined above.

Theoretical framework

The forecasting procedure and the resulting analyses are based on a systematic view of transportation. It is therefore necessary to embed air transport forecasting and simulation in a framework of relevant relationships that take into account the whole transport market as well as demographic, economic, political, spatial and technical components. A modelling process based on these interrelationships explains the transport market by multimodal and multi-sector determinants. This approach ensures the consistency of the whole model system in every step of the simulation process as the models always process balanced figures of all endogenous measures. Hence, no transport activity appears or disappears unexplained within the system. Changes in the system's state are substitutive or complementary and synergetic effects lead to new situations concerning diversion, accessibility or attractiveness. These effects can be analysed with respect to modes (e.g. road, rail, sea, and air) and/or trip purposes (e.g. business, vacation, private).

In the light of the complexity outlined in the previous sections of this chapter it is obvious that there must be a sequence of models dealing with all the interrelationships and dependencies to catch the consumers' behaviour. The system approach developed is based on the classical 4 step procedure, namely generation, distribution, modal split and assignment. There are some differences in combining steps, modelling techniques, functional form and additional modelling steps to cope with specific effects within air transport. The following figure shows the principle structure.

Figure 3.2. **Sequence of models for air transport forecasting**

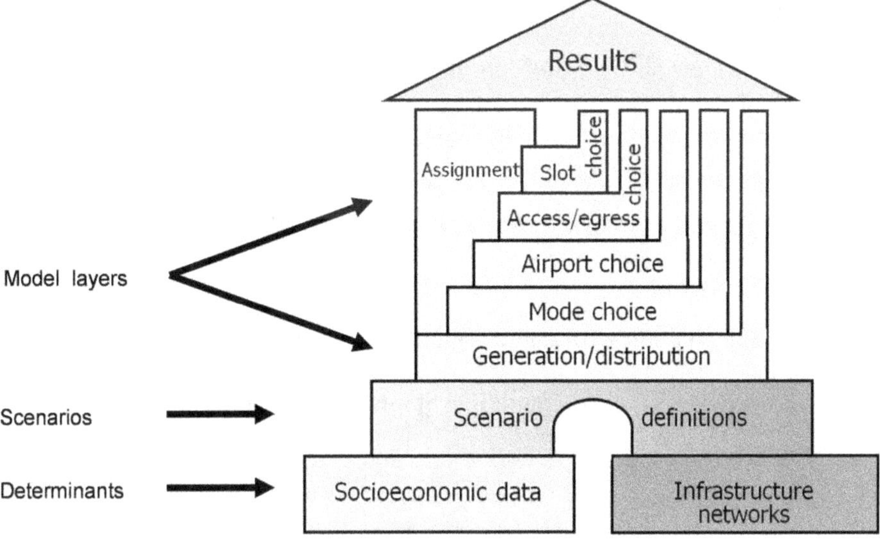

The basis of all models contains the determinants of transport. It is the database where all information is stored to run the models, e.g. socio-economy, regional attractors, networks. The second block defines the scenarios to be tested. Short-term scenarios are often used to execute ex post[11] forecasts investigating a specific question, e.g. changes in network, competition, air service agreements or taxation. Long-term scenarios are mainly used for ex-ante forecasts and contain a series of assumptions such as socio-economic development, infrastructure investments, capacity constraints, airline strategies or policy measures. In principle the scenario definitions can encompass all input data for the models and any measures with quantitative influence on the model variables. The richness of a scenario definition depends on the level of granulation the models determine.

The first modelling block concerns the generation-distribution model. It computes the total traffic volumes, where they emerge and whereto they are directed. There are models splitting the demand and the distribution of traffic, whereby first the mobility pattern and then the demand distribution is computed. Here we follow the combined generation-distribution approach to incorporate in parallel the substitution and complementarities of destinations and to deal with the requirement of spatial competition. In the following the principle mathematical form is displayed (for more details see Gaudry, Mandel and Rothengatter, (1994a) and Gaudry, Mandel and Rothengatter, (1994b)).

The flow T from region i to region j is computed by a non-linear function g^d with socio-economic factors A (a= 1, ..., A) and the modes utility, e.g. network impedances, U (m=1, ..., M) as follows:

$$T_{ij} = g^d(\{A_{ij_a}\},\{U_{ij_m}\}) \quad \text{with} \quad A_{ij_a} \equiv \left[S_{i_a}^{1/2} S_{j_a}^{1/2} \right]$$

whereby S reflects variables like GDP, population, purchase power, income and

$$U_{ij_m} = e^{v_{ij_m}}$$

whereby v is an additive non-linear function of network impedances like time and distance under consideration of all modes and consumer related data like age and gender.

As regression problem one can formulate the above into a simple multiplicative form, such as:

$$T_{ij} = \beta_0 A_{ij_1}^{\beta_1} \ldots . A_{ij_A}^{\beta_A} U_{ij}^{\beta_U} u_{ij}$$

To detect and gain the non-linear effects Box-Cox transformations (BCT) of the strictly positive variables are applied. To guarantee for a constant variance a variable correcting heteroscedasticity is imposed. The error term is analysed under consideration of non-linearity (BCT) to extract functional information so that a pure stochastic term is left.

The functional form is enriched by a vector describing the dependencies of neighbouring regions as destination of a trip so that one can cope with the problem of irrelevance of spatial competition which is inherent due to Luce's IIA axiom.

Given the following situation we assume region 2 and region 7 to be close substitutes.

Figure 3.3. **Spatial competition**

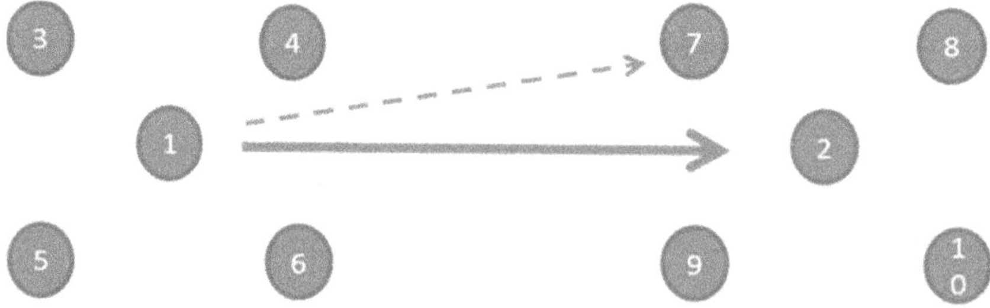

Under consideration of this spatial competition Tij looks like:

$$T_{12} = f(A_{12}, A_{17}, U_{12}, U_{17}) + \upsilon_{12}$$

$$T_{17} = f(A_{12}, A_{17}, U_{12}, U_{17}) + \upsilon_{17}$$

Now all competing regions (below denoted with index k) influence the attractiveness of the flow between i and j, hence competition among regions is introduced which can lead to substitutive but as well to complementary effects in the choice of destination.

$$T_{ij} = \rho T_{ik} + \beta(U_{ij} - \rho U_{ik}) + \omega_{ij}$$

For more details about the spatial competition it is recommended to read the article 'Introducing Spatial Competition through an Autoregressive Contiguous Distributed (AR-C-D) Process in Intercity Generation-Distribution Models within a Quasi-Direct Format (QDF)' available on www.mkm.de .

The next modelling steps concern the consumer's choice on transport mode, access to and egress from the airport, choice of airport, route, and slot. A modal choice model (Mandel, 1992) is used to identify the consumer's elasticity with respect to the alternative transport modes air, rail and road. Especially for countries or areas with a dense highway network and available high speed rail services the competition among modes is considered to be essential. But this leads directly to the next choice problem of the consumer: How to approach the airport? Excellent high-speed rail connections from and to an airport can increase the catchment area significantly allowing convenient access or egress from more distant communities. This influences the slot, airport and route choice as well which all together explain the consumers' selection of services (Mandel, 1999a).

While the first modelling step concerns the generation – distribution calculation allowing the construction of a matrix of traffic flows between the regions in focus, the second model level splits the amount of travellers detected between modes, access-egress options, airports, routes and slots. Depending on the underlying data one can apply share or probabilistic models whereby the estimation algorithms differ but the principle remains the same. In the following the principle is outlined by using a share model, which is based on aggregated observations for the mode choice problem.

The share of travellers using mode m on relation i j (denoted as t=1, ...,i , ..., I) is equal to the attractiveness v of mode m on relation t in context of the sum attractiveness of all modes p (p=1, ..., M) on relation t. So it is just the relative attractiveness of one mode in respect to the one of all potential available modes. This is expressed by:

$$sh(m)_t = \frac{e^{v_{m_t}}}{\sum_{p=1}^{M} e^{v_{p_t}}} \quad \text{with} \quad v_{m_i} = \beta_{0_m} + \sum_n \beta_n N_{n_i}^{(\lambda_{x_n})} + \sum_a \beta_a S_{a_i} + \sum_p \beta_p P_{p_i}$$

whereby N are network characteristics, e.g. time, cost, frequency (where λ indicates non-linearity which is discussed later), S are socio-economic characteristics, e.g. age-class, gender, employment, household size, income and P are characteristics of the trip purpose, e.g. trip duration, business.

Alternatively probability models based on disaggregate observations can be formulated in the same way. The probability of an individual traveller n choosing a mode i is expressed as follows:

$$P(i)_n = \frac{U_{in}}{\sum_j U_{jn}} \quad i, j \in C_n \text{ with } U_{in} = e^{\left(\beta_i x_i + \sum_{k=1}^{K} \beta_{ki} x_{kin}\right)}$$

Where U is expressing the utility of the mode n experienced by individual i or j (denoted as m) and X refers to the N, S and P characteristics stated above. Both forms are of simple logistic form reflecting the proportion of one alternative to all others, whereby the dependent variable is given by an observed share of demand an alternative attracted or alternatively the dependent variable is an individual decision of a consumer for an alternative out of a set of alternatives. The latter usually is extracted from an individual survey.

Assuming observations, samples and all other necessary input data are perfect so that the models fulfil all criteria mentioned before, it is essential to know what type of functional form the models use. Analysis based travel surveys and traffic counting show that consumer choices are not represent linear relationships. For example the value of marginal time savings is a function of total travel time; similarly, modal choice becomes inelastic after a certain distance and passenger may have a bias towards one mode compared to another.

The mathematical form of a model has to allow for adjustments of the curvature measured on the base of observations. Such additional degrees of freedom must be estimated simultaneously so that each characteristic describing an alternative is weighted correctly in relationship to all other characteristics to reflect the balance of its influence upon the traveller properly. The degrees of freedom mentioned concern the non-linearity and the captivity of the functional form. Their importance is apparent when considering how LCCs have reduced the income threshold for air travel, or how limited vacation time may prevent a trip from being extended even if the consumer could afford to do so.

The models shown above imply a linear functional form. In consequence the effect of a given difference in transport conditions is independent of the service level characteristics so that the response curve to changes in service characteristics is symmetric with respect to its inflection point. But as outlined the traveller's behaviour is non-linear. Thresholds influence the decision and activate changes in product choice.

Therefore the functional form must be flexible so that one can circumvent linearity in variables and consider the level of the variable. To introduce the non-linearity different possibilities exist. E.g. the Box-Cox transformation can be applied for strictly positive variables:

$$BC: x^{(\lambda)} = \begin{cases} (x^{\lambda_k} - 1)/\lambda_k & \lambda_k \neq 0 \\ \ln(x) & \lambda_k = 0 \end{cases} \text{ for}$$

The BC transformation applied on the probability model leads to the following form:

$$P(i)_n = \frac{e^{(\beta_i x_i + \sum_{k=1}^{K} \beta_{ki} x_{kin}^{(\lambda_{ki})})}}{\sum_j e^{(\beta_j x_j + \sum_{k=1}^{K} \beta_{kj} x_{kjn}^{(\lambda_{kj})})}}$$

The following figure shows the different curvatures of the linear Logit function and the ones with transformations applied on a positive variable (Mandel, Gaudry and Rothengatter, 1994). The range of thresholds is with the asymmetric tail of the function and indicates the change of travel time where people start to reconsider their behaviour over-proportionally.

When looking at the linear and BC-Logit curvature it has to be noted that the choice probabilities go to zero (one) when the representative utility V_i goes to $-\infty$ ($+\infty$) so that (see figure above) one cannot model thick tails due to specification error, modeller ignorance, compulsive consumption or captivity to alternatives. To bypass this constraint, the captivity of consumers, the Box-Tukey transformation can be used:

$$BT: \quad x^{(\lambda,\mu)} = \begin{cases} ((x_k - \mu_k)^{\lambda_k} - 1)/\lambda_k & \text{with} \quad \lambda_k \neq 0, (x_k + \mu_k) > 0 \\ \ln(x_k + \mu_k) & \lambda_k = 0, (x_k + \mu_k) > 0 \end{cases}$$

The BT transformation applied on the probability model leads to the following form:

$$P(i)_n = \frac{e^{(\beta_i x_i + \sum_{k=1}^{K} \beta_{ki} x_{kin}^{(\lambda_{ki}, \mu_{ki})})}}{\sum_j e^{(\beta_j x_j + \sum_{k=1}^{K} \beta_{kj} x_{kjn}^{(\lambda_{kj}, \mu_{kj})})}}$$

In the figure below it can be seen that there are about 20% inelastic captive riders who are forced to use the displayed alternative irrespective of any changes in the variable, e.g. long-haul business travellers. The μ coefficient allows the function to converge to a certain level at both sides of the function.

Figure 3.4. **Functional forms**

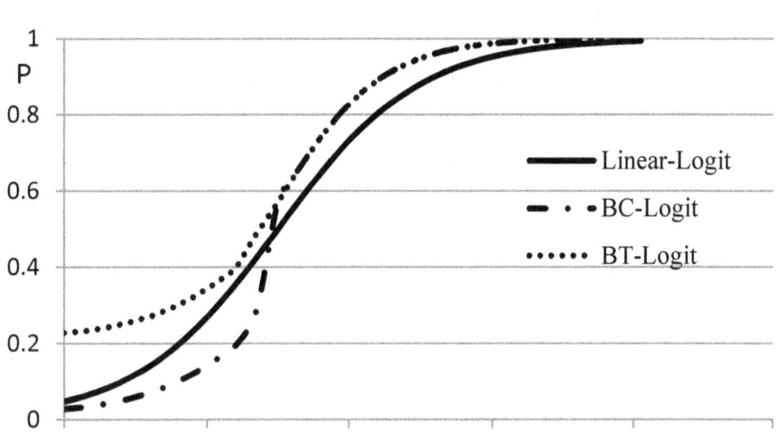

A linear functional form which considers captivities is available when choosing the Dogit model. But also a Box-Cox transformation can be applied in parallel. This allows catching captive riders in combination with non-linearity of variables. This form looks as follows:

$$P(i)_n = \frac{e^{(\beta_i x_i + \sum_{k=1}^{K} \beta_{ki} x_{kin}^{(\lambda_{ki})})} + \theta_{in} \sum_j e^{(\beta_j x_j + \sum_{k=1}^{K} \beta_{kj} x_{kjn}^{(\lambda_{kj})})}}{(1 + \sum_j \theta_{jn}) \sum_j e^{(\beta_j x_j + \sum_{k=1}^{K} \beta_{kj} x_{kjn}^{(\lambda_{kj})})}}$$

Within the system approach outlined the technique of choice modelling described is used for all the choice problems mentioned.

Up to now the models are independent from each other and to encounter the effects from one decision level respectively model level to the other one has to link the modelling steps by the quasi-direct format (QDF) (Gaudry et al., 1998) using the representative utility function of the lower level models in the upper ones as an additional independent explanatory variable, which is called modal utility index. This link ensures consistency of behaviour across the system approach.

For example the quasi direct format is explained for the generation-distribution model which includes the modal utility index, respectively denominator, of the modal split model as an independent characteristic in the mathematical expression of the problem in focus.

$$QDF: T_{ij}^{m} = T_{ij} \cdot S_{ij}^{m} = T_{ij} \cdot \sum_{j} e^{(\beta_j x_j + \sum_{k=1}^{K} \beta_{kj} x_{kjn}^{(\lambda_{kj})})}$$

The linkage of the model levels is a prerequisite for the reflection of the interdependencies within the decision process of a consumer (Mandel, 1999b). This may concerns the relationship of the consumer's choice and travel demand, competition of modes (multi-modality – rail-road-air-sea), the co-operation of modes (inter-modality – transport chains across modes like rail & fly, sea-road), and the competition within a transport mode system (intra-modality – e.g. selection of different routes including various transfer hubs and airports at the origin and destination). An example is how high speed rail services like the TGV significantly reduced air traffic between Paris and Lyon, Brussels or Strasbourg but also fed long-haul traffic from these cities into Paris Charles de Gaulle airport. A similar situation took place in Frankfurt, where high speed rail replaced short haul flights but increased the catchment area of the airport for long haul flights.

Another aspect addressed concerns the traveller's elasticity. For all expressions one can derive this measure such as the point elasticity:

$$\eta(S(i)_n, x_{kin}) = \frac{\partial S(i)_n}{\partial x_{kin}} \frac{x_{kin}}{S(i)_n}$$

It is just the derivation of the function for a certain variable. As a result a ceteris paribus variation of the demand for alternative i by a 1% change of the characteristic value of alternative i can be computed. So market effects can be analysed when changing supply characteristics, e.g. reducing the price of an alternative, increasing the service frequency or introducing a new service.

In principle the whole system approach can be expressed as a function of elasticity, such as:

$$\eta(T_i, x_k) = \eta(T, x_k) + \eta(P(\text{mode})_n, x_k) + \eta(P(airport)_n, x_k) + \eta(P(access/egress)_n, x_k) + \eta(P(timeslice)_n, x_k) + \eta(P(airline)_n, x_k)$$

or in simplified notification:

$$\eta(alternative) = \eta(total\ flow) + \eta(\text{mode}) + \eta(airport) + \eta(access/egress) + \eta(time\ slice) + \eta(airline)$$

This set of elasticities measures (Mandel, 1999c) competition within the transport system and the model can be interpreted as a cascade of elasticity.

Finally, procedures are required to compute impediments reflecting the attractiveness of each alternative based on the infrastructure networks of all modes. The different algorithms used cope with the specifics of the modes. Schedules for air transport are considered at a fairly granular level so a connection builder has to be used which considers flights, airlines, alliances, code shares, time zones and connecting times at airports as well as access-egress time. It is recommended to develop a tailor made procedure to optimise the algorithm so that it can cope with the problem addressed in harmony with the available computer processing power, whereby parallel processing should be kept in mind to minimise run time. The impedances computed need to contain the network path information to allow an assignment of the traffic demand.

Please note that the methodological description provided is an overview, it is recommended to look at the further references available from: www.mkm.de section publications/papers.

It follows that once demand forecast is executed aircraft movements differentiated by weight classes, schedule, or peak day analyses can be derived. For air cargo an equivalent approach is developed.

Reflection of the status quo as reference point and scenario simulation

The analysis of the forecast can be based on an ex-post or ex-ante scenario. For ex-post analysis the basic framework data for a reference year is are available from national statistical offices or commercial sources like schedules. For an ex-ante scenario data will have to be worked out for the specific year to be forecasted.

The ex-post forecasts can be used in two ways. First of all the representation of a given reference year is important to validate the systems. This is done through a matrix bounding approach and has to be executed first when setting up the system in order to ensure reliable results. The principle procedure is depicted in the following figure

The calibration is an iterative process where data from various sources and model results are assessed to detect irregularities, inconsistencies and errors. The arrows symbolise the principle process flow, while the recursive parts and their nesting are not displayed due to their complexity.

Let's assume a model set is available as well as all the necessary input data to complete a run (see the blue coloured boxes in the following figure). As result of a ceteris paribus model run for the reference year one receives an ex-post forecast. These model results are validated by independent data sources like national statistics, link counts, surveys, etc. to identify irregularities, inconsistencies and errors. They are investigated by checking input data, procedures, programmes and models whereby errors are corrected – in the worst case even by setting up new model estimations. This step is essential to ensure that model results are reflecting reality at an objective reference case or a base year respectively. This enhances market transparency and displays a full market picture of a previous year, which is used to benchmark demand effects which can be investigated as ex post forecasts. It is crucial to understand the competitive situation stakeholders are in.

Figure 3.5. **Validation, calibration and simulation**

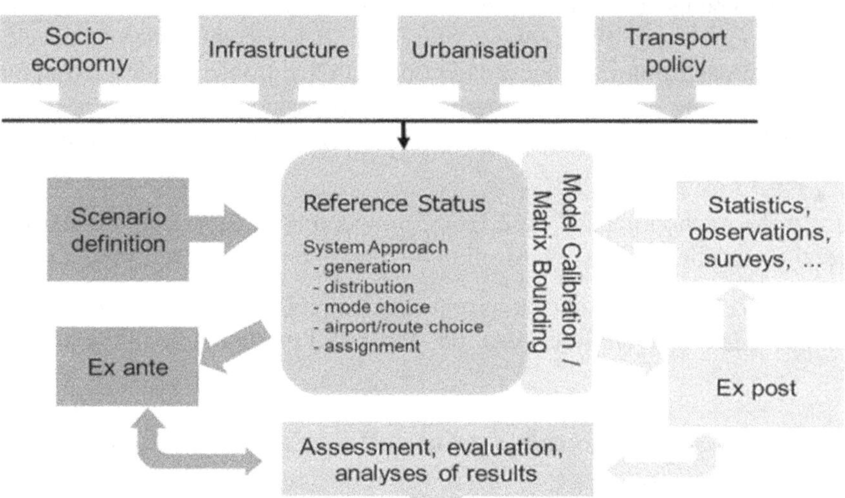

The second possibility of ex-post analysis can be used to estimate the counterfactual. One can investigate policy or strategic actions without bias.

In addition market potentials of new routes can be investigated under ceteris paribus conditions of the existing market. A successive scan of new air services (SONAR) identifies, evaluates, and ranks all technically possible routes from a defined airport. It takes into account the offers of all competing airports and their catchment areas. The SONAR procedure implements the best identified routes in the simulation system and integrates them into an actual flight schedule. Finally, the passenger potential is calculated. The system allows optimising the existing flight services, if passenger potential is not yet being fully exploited. Interdependencies between new and existing services in the air transport system as a whole are fully considered. As a result, one gets revenues by route and, coupled with information on costs, the most profitable routes for a certain airport. Both network and aircraft fleets can be optimised using the same approach, just the internal routines need to be rearranged.

The ex-ante forecasts allow a wide range of scenario simulations. Any change of the transport determinants described within the framework conditions can be applied and will lead to results. Whether one or several of determinants changes does not matter for the system approach as all influencing factors will interact consistently according to the linkage of all the econometric models used. Therefore a scenario can consider the effects of e.g. implementation of kerosene tax, the establishment of a new airport, the installation of new high speed rail services and a change of the home base carrier's network strategy at the same time. Obviously network dynamics as well as more complex socio-economic interrelations are covered across all modes, (e.g. the effects of regional differences in purchase power or geo-metrics and the interrelationship of mobility and oil price).

For the different model stages some examples of scenario elements are listed below:

- **Generation – distribution of traffic:**
  - Socio-economic framework data (e.g. population, trade, GDP, oil).
  - Political decisions (e.g. taxes, security, noise charges).
  - Regional attractiveness (e.g. type of region, temperature, sea, mountains).
  - Political decisions (e.g. traffic rights, subsidies).

- **Mode choice:**
  - Network/Service characteristics (e.g. time, cost, frequency, transfer, operation days).
  - Political decisions (e.g. public service obligation (PSO), infrastructure investments).
- **Airport / Route choice:**
  - Service-Structure (e.g. new route / closure, minimum connecting times (MCT), airline base, transfer node).
  - Infrastructure (e.g. access / egress by surface modes, inter-modal routes).
- **Assignment:**
  - Infrastructure networks (e.g. new airports, new high speed rail (HSR) services) and/or changes in network attributes (e.g. capacity, speed, charges, tolls, fees).

Finally it has to be noted that the approach outlined is not just focused on one airport, in principle scenarios can cover multiple airports and in consequence considers the interdependencies.

Complexity and coverage

A realistic picture of transport activities requires capturing the consumers' situation in greatest possible detail. Therefore, the starting point concerns the location of the travellers themselves rather than the airport of choice, and their desired destination. Transport flows have to be modelled from door to door rather than from one airport to another.

The approach described here uses the NUTS 3 level[12] (nomenclature of territorial units for statistics) for the European member states for representation of the location of travellers origin and destination, while the rest of the world is covered by larger zones based on administrative boundaries at NUTS 2, 1 or 0 level (in total about 2 300 regions). The approach therefore considers all traffic within, to, from, and across Europe.

All the mode specific networks have to be compatible with this level of detail. So the road network consists of links down to the third order of streets (ca. 2.8 Mio. links) and the rail network considers rail services according to the published schedules reflecting different service types. The air mode considers all airports with published services based on HAFAS[13] within Europe, plus more than 200 representative airports for the rest of the world. Of course the air services are reflected as published in the schedules but need to be enriched by charter services or LCC services which are not covered by the commercial schedule providers. The underlying demand data framework must be representative (and highly valuable) for all commercial traffic.

To cope with intra-modality when considering competing hubs the route and airport choice models must consider a sufficient number of intercontinental and continental alternatives. Only a combination of detailed regional network representation makes a model flexible enough to deal with the network dynamics of the transport market. The results of the system approach are dynamic, e.g. the catchment of an airport depends on the air services offered at all competing airports and can be different for each route and passenger segment.

Application of the KMmetric model

This section highlights the capabilities of the existing MKmetric tool using the modal approach described above,, with special focus on airport and route choice. The base year for the analysis is 2012.

Airport choice

The nucleus of the model is the airport choice based oon consumers' behaviour. A passenger decides on the travel alternatives for a given trip. This decision is based on the individual's weighting of the attributes for each travel alternative. In the model this weighting results in the calculation of choice probabilities assigned to the distinct route alternatives.

The following figure displays the sixteen travel options available within the simulation model between the city of Bremen, Germany, and the centre region of Thailand, around Bangkok and the choice probabilities on them for non-business-travellers.

Seven of the route alternatives start from the nearest airport Bremen (BRE) to the region of origin. As there are no direct flights between BRE and BKK, all options require a transfer at one hub, from which flights to BRE as well as to BKK are provided, namely Amsterdam (AMS), Paris (CDG), Frankfurt (FRA), Istanbul (IST), Munich (MUC) and Zurich (ZRH), of which the one via FRA is the mostly chosen (17.2%).

In addition there are also travel options available from other airports: Düsseldorf (DUS), Hamburg (HAM) and Hannover (HAJ), from which a flight to Bangkok is possible nonstop (from DUS and FRA) or via hubs to which no flights from BRE are offered, e.g. like those from the Gulf carriers Etihad at Abu Dhabi (AUH) or Emirates at Dubai (DXB). From all these options the share of the one to go by surface transport to FRA and take a nonstop flight to BKK from there has the second largest share in this market (14%), a result of the excellent accessibility of Frankfurt airport by high speed rail.

Figure 3.6. **Airport choice for a trip from Bremen to Bangkok**

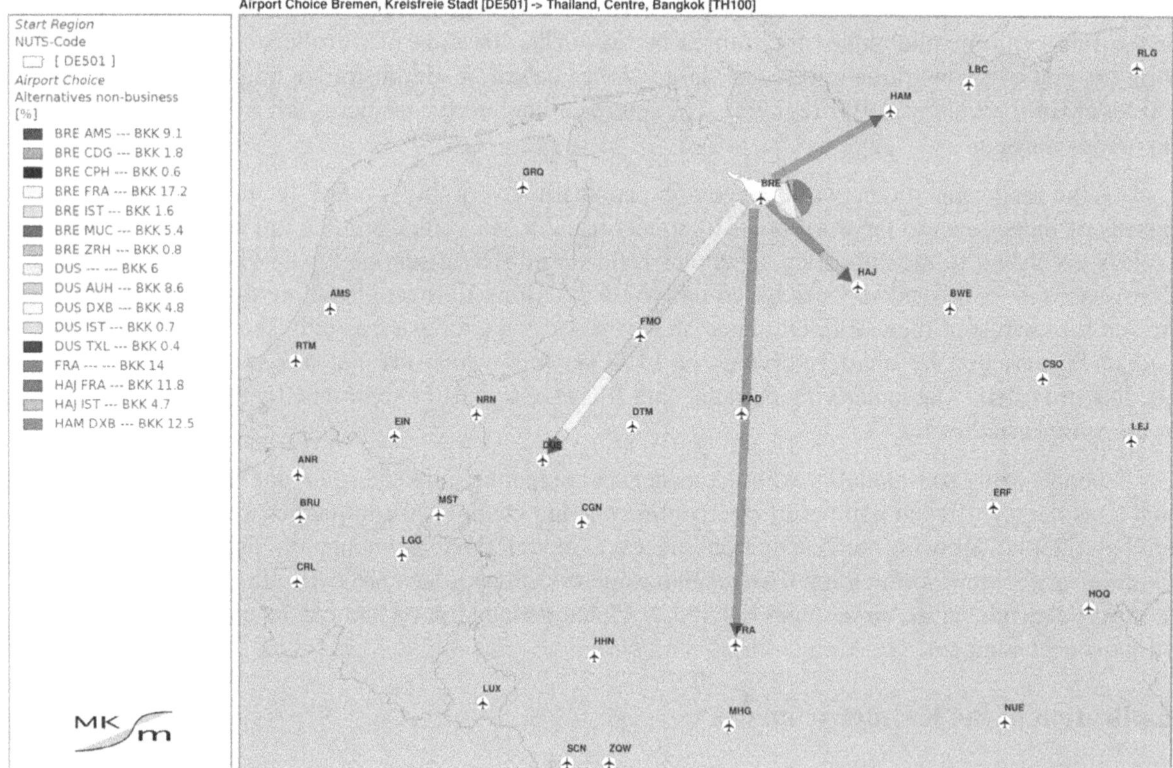

Route competitors

Similar to the airport choice analysis as mentioned before, this example displays the different routes which compete for a distinct O-D market. As input for the analysis we have chosen the airports of Sao Paulo (GRU), Brazil and Tokyo Narita (NRT), Japan and a limitation of the catchment area of both airports by 120 minutes of access-egress time.

The figure displays the most relevant route chosen between those regions, from which the airports mentioned can be reached within 2 hours by surface transport. The routes are coloured in line with the number of passengers travelling on each of them. The routes considered do not necessarily all link the airports of GRU and NRT.

As GRU and NRT are more or less antipodes to each other (greater circle distance is at about 18 500 km), there are eastbound as well as westbound travel options.

The westbound travel-options displayed, which in this case take the core of demand withal require a plane change at an US-airport. The route via Dallas Fort Worth (DFW) is the most important of them, attracting more than 40 000 passengers, while the others, e.g. via New York's John F. Kennedy Airport (JFK), Chicago (ORD), Newark (EWR) or Washington (IAD), have smaller shares on the total demand (≈100 000 passengers as sum of both directions). Minor passenger flows (not displayed) on this O-D pair occur via San Francisco, Houston and Toronto, Canada.

In the eastbound direction, the routes from GRU via the European airports Paris (CDG), Frankfurt (FRA), Munich (MUC) and Rome (FCO) to Tokyo are the most relevant travel options. While most of them are heading to Tokyo's Narita airport (NRT), there is also a second option when travelling via CDG: instead of flying to Narita, via Paris it has also been possible to travel to or from Tokyo's Haneda Airport (HND).

Figure 3.7. **Route competitors for the route GRU - NRT**

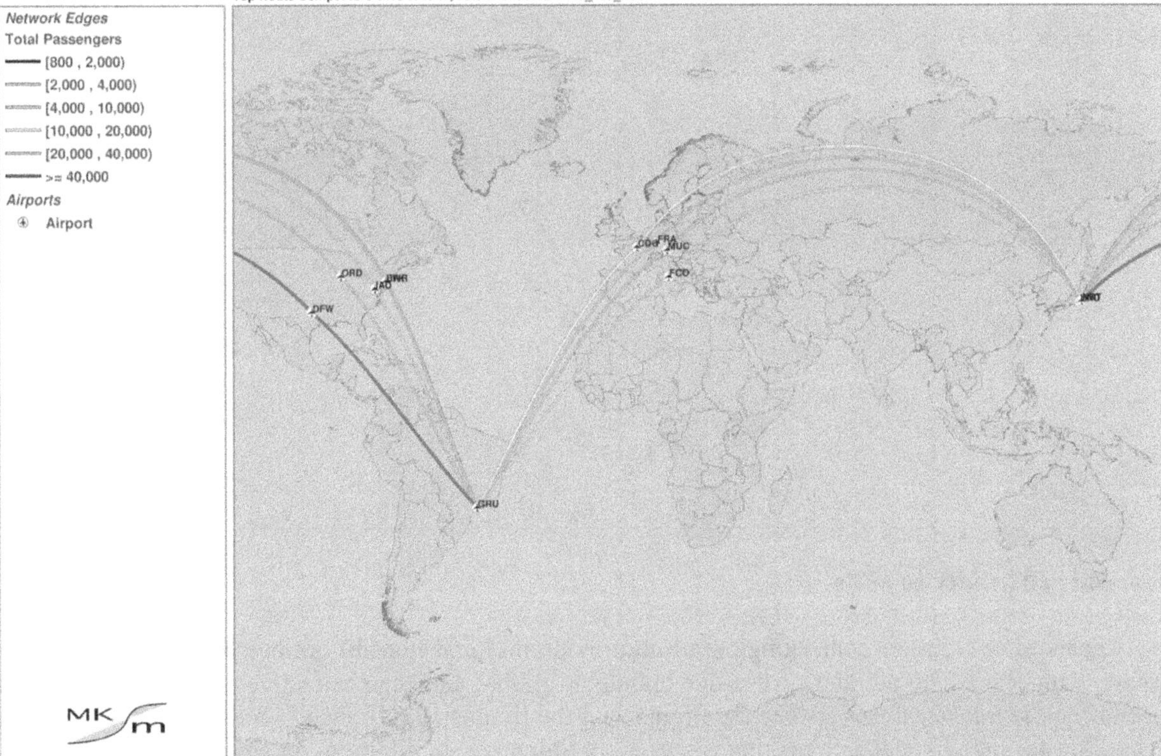

Flight segments

After calculating all route choices for every pair of origin or destination regions, and enriching them with the underlying passenger flows on a regional basis, it is possible to assign them either to distinct flight segments or to sequences of them. One possible analysis of such an assigned air network is to examine the true origin, destination and routing of passengers on a given flight leg. For example, results for a flight between Hamburg (HAM) and Dubai (DXB) on Emirates Airlines are displayed in the following picture. While the number of passengers, which entered at HAM from another flight, is minimal, a vast majority of passengers originally starting to fly from HAM do not have their final destination at DXB, but transfer there for other destinations, either in the Middle East, in South-East Asia, Oceania or in Eastern and Southern part of Africa. Also those passengers, travelling between the city of Bremen and Thailand that we had identified in the airport choice analysis, are part of the passenger volumes displayed below.

It should be mentioned that this type of analysis is not only feasible for existing routes, furthermore it can be used to identify the acquirable demand for new routes to be implemented into an existing air network and point out the routes' passenger potential concerning local traffic as well as the number of transfer passengers who would use a new route.

Figure 3.8. **Passenger diversity on the flight segment HAM – DXB**

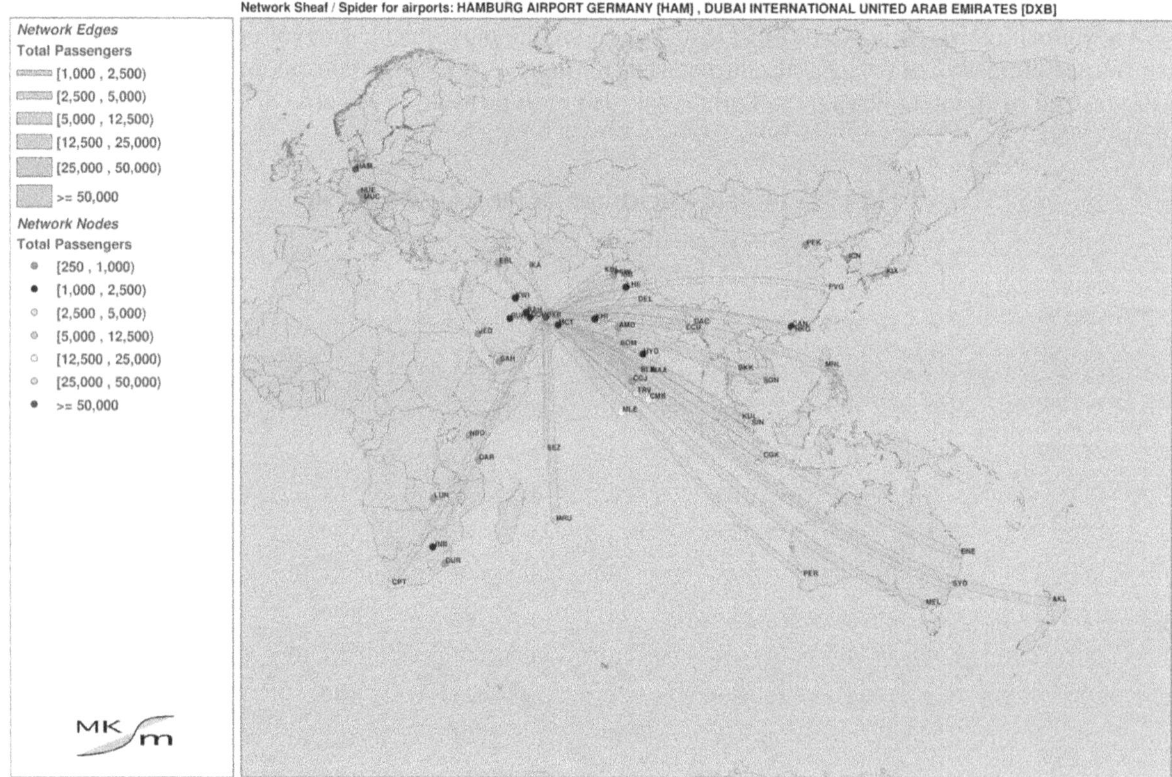

Demand sensitivity to slots

Routes to or from, or connecting to, a hub provide multiple transfer options on one or both of the airports connected. The amount of transfer options available and their attractiveness for the consumer depends on the transfer time between the flights, and the frequency of transfer options. Long layovers or scarce transfer options make competing routes more attractive. In addition, on an airlines point of view not only the absolute number of transfer passengers matter, but also their total travel distance, as the revenues received from an intercontinental passenger are higher than those from a short-haul passenger.

To tackle this complexity the analysis uses 'weighted connectivity'. The weighted connectivity for a specific route takes into account all transfer options available for each distinct slot at one of the airports connected by the route, weighted by the duration between an arrival at this slot and the next available departure time for each different transfer destination. In addition each of these transfer options are weighted by the passenger potential from the considered routes' origin to each transfer destination. In the following pictures the analysis for the existing route between Seoul (ICN) and Prague (PRG), either for PRG and in the second picture for ICN is shown.

Figure 3.9. **Passenger demand sensitivity to the air service Seoul – Prague**

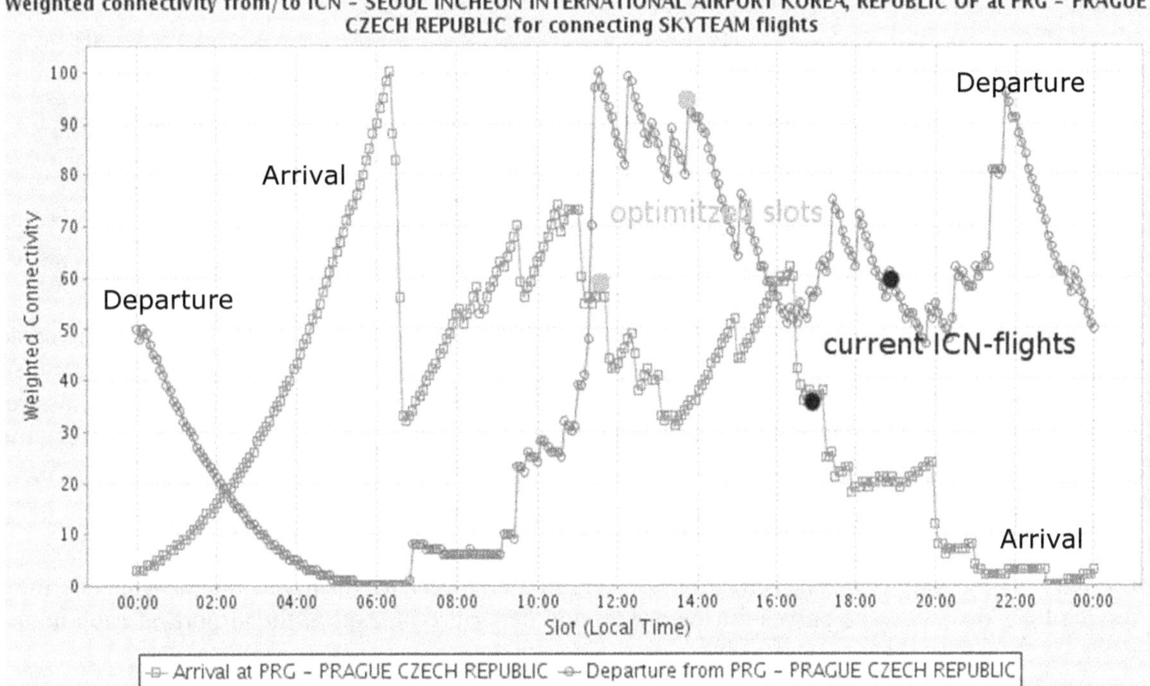

Arrival/departure from ICN at PRG versus demand

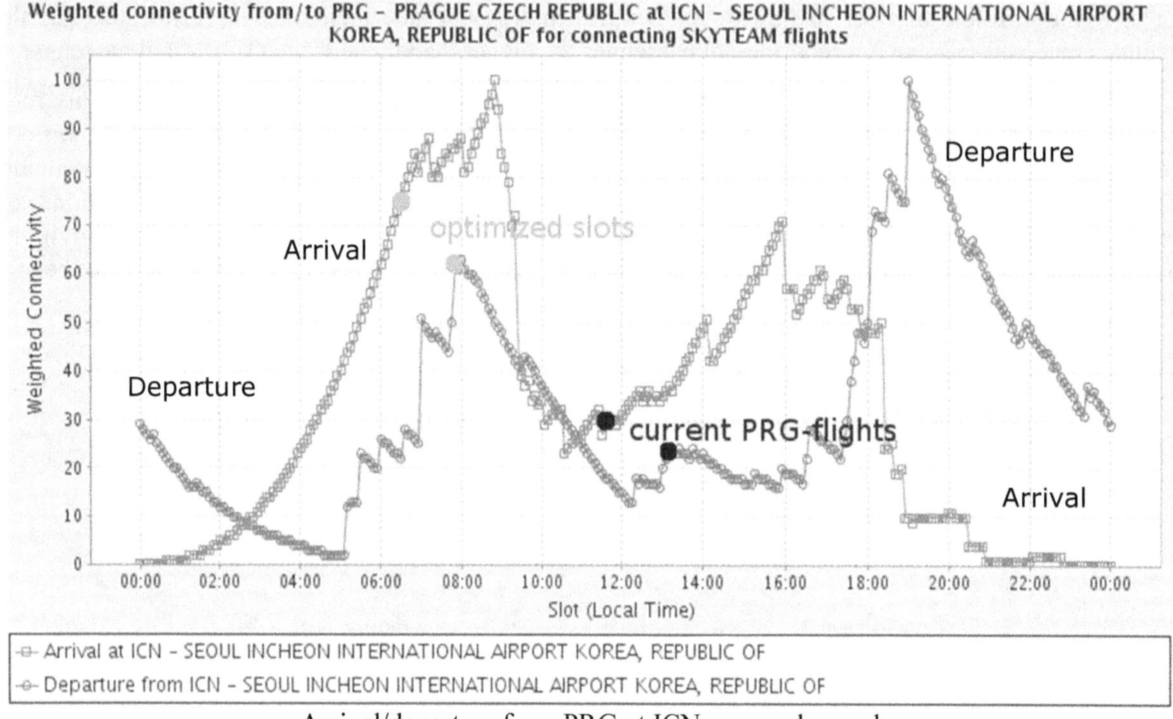

Arrival/departure from PRG at ICN versus demand

This connectivity analysis neglects transfer options requiring a detour compared to existing nonstop flight options. For example when doing a weighted connectivity analysis for the route PRG-ICN, transfer options for Abu Dhabi (AUH) are neglected, as AUH is available nonstop from PRG as well as from ICN and flying from ICN via PRG to the Middle East (or even worse from PRG via ICN to AUH) would mean an enormous detour compared to the existing nonstop flights.

Also the minimum connecting times for the airports connected were taken into account. The values calculated are on an index base with a value of 100 for that arrival / departure slot offering maximum connectivity. These graphs shows vertically the weighted connectivity results of the pre-analysis for an air service for a distinct route curves for the arrival and departure indexes at the airport at each hour of the day.

So when marking the current arrival / departure times for the route considered in PRG and as well in ICN (black spots), one can see that, the slots chosen do not provide the maximum connectivity possible at both airports (index values of 20/30 at ICN and 60/35 at PRG). But when operating the flights about four to five hours earlier, i.e. stop at PRG around lunch time instead of late afternoon and arrive/depart at ICN in the morning instead of midday, would lead to a significant higher connectivity for these flights, resulting in index values of 60/90 at PRG and 75/60 at ICN.

This analysis can also be used, as a pre-step procedure to identify an optimal schedule for a route to be examined in the simulation model.

Dynamic catchment

It was outlined in the airport choice section, that consumers may chose a starting airport which is quite distant form their region, if its accessibility is good and the flight options offered there (e.g. nonstop flights) are not available from the airport which is closest to their region with a significant probability. For the question of the size of an airports' catchment this means, that such a catchment can be defined neither by just drawing a circle in a distinct distance around this airport, nor that all regions within a specific isochrone "belong" to an airport exclusively, while other regions strictly can be assigned to other airports. To point this out, the catchment of an airport for two different destination markets is displayed and all regions from which an airport can attract passengers are coloured.

Figure 3.10. **Catchment of Frankfurt for destinations in the far east**

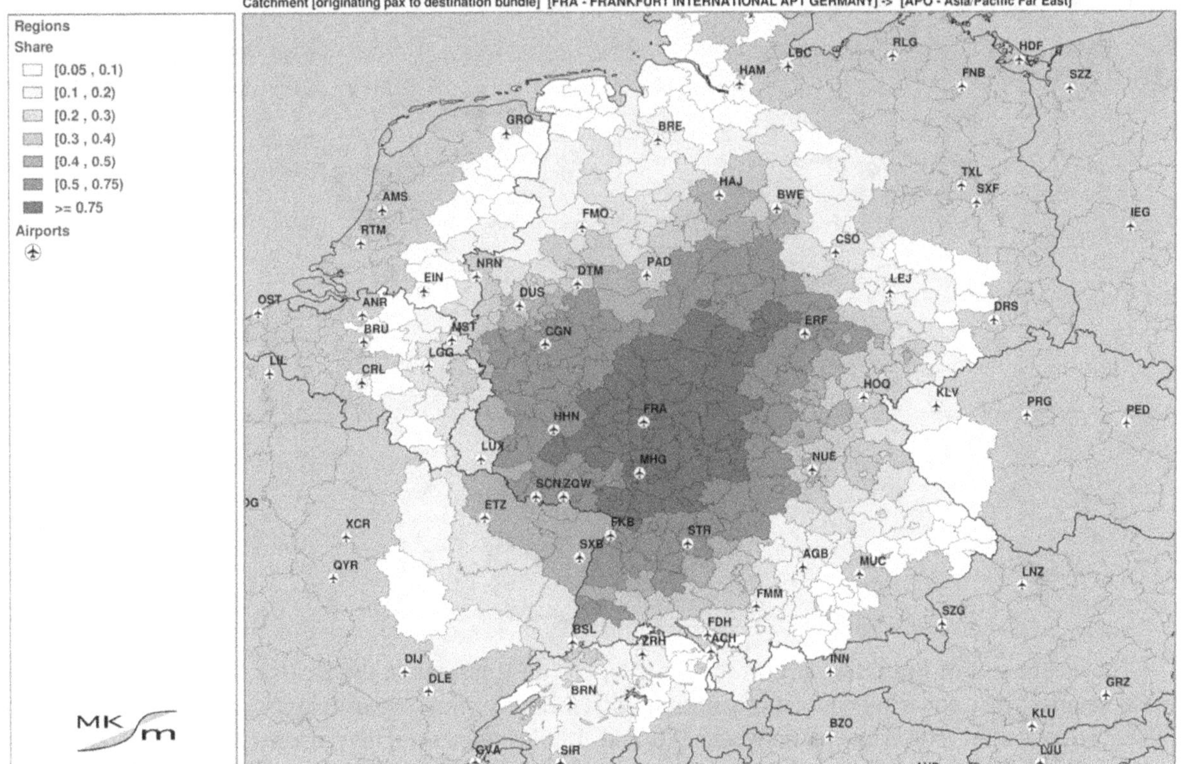

The different shades from light to dark reflect the market share the airport considered has in the specific region. Market share in this context means: if an airport can attract 24 out of 100 passengers from a region, while the 76 others chose different airports to start their trip, the market share of the airport considered in this region is 24%. Regions from which the airport can attract less than 5% of all passengers are displayed in grey.

In the figure above, the market share of Frankfurt airport for destinations in the far-east are depicted. On basis of regions where Frankfurt can achieve a market share of at least 5%, the area stretches from the very north of Germany to Switzerland and the most western part of Austria in the south, covering a distance of about 1 000 kilometres. In the east-west direction, parts of the Netherlands, Belgium, France and Luxembourg belong to this catchment, which reaches in east Saxony and even that part of the Czech Republic bordering to Germany – in total a distance of more than 600 kilometres is covered in this direction. The provision of nonstop flights to numerous destinations in the market considered, of which the most are not available from other airports in the close or larger vicinity of Frankfurt, with some of them even exclusively provided at Frankfurt for the European continent and the excellent connection of FRA with high speed rail services, are the reason for this huge catchment concerning the far east market.

Figure 3.11. **Catchment of Frankfurt for destinations in the British Isles**

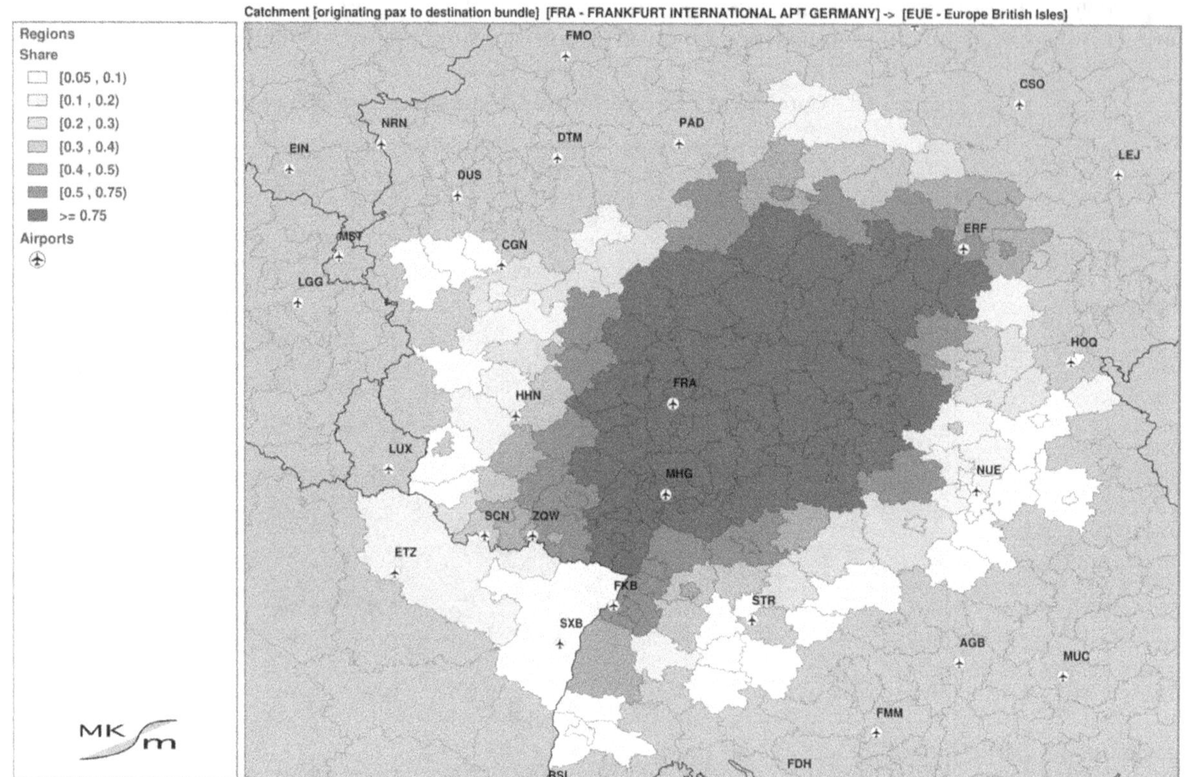

The catchment of Frankfurt airport for travellers to destinations in the British Isles is very different: by far smaller, just covering the central regions of Germany plus some neighbouring *départements* in France, with a total extension of between 300 and 500 kilometres. The reason for this in comparison quite small catchment area is that the destination portfolio of most airports surrounding Frankfurt covers at least one of the London airports and in many cases also quite a few other destinations in the UK or in Ireland.

Such analyses allow an airport to identify quite well where its core markets are or where it might be worthwhile to put more marketing efforts, but it gives little indication in regions where another airport is a serious competitor. In these cases it is useful to display simultaneously the catchment areas of two different (competing) airports in one graph. As an example, this analysis is displayed in figure 3.12 for the two airports of Geneva (GVA), Switzerland and Lyon (LYS), France, both with quite a few international and even a limited number of intercontinental flights in their destination portfolios. Different colours (shades of grey) indicate different splits of travellers using Lyon, Geneva or other neighbouring airports (the darkest areas show 100% of travellers using other airports). The Rhône-Alpes area directly between GVA and LYS (lightest grey) sees heavy competition between the two airports, with a 50:50 split of travellers.

When rendered in colour the figure reveals the market domination of GVA, which not only covers the northern part of the Lac Leman area, but also the French regions south of Geneva with their ski resorts, while the focus of LYS, beside the city of Lyon, lies more in serving areas to the south down to Avignon, from where the influence of the Marseille airport (MRS) dominates the market.

Figure 3.12. **Competition between Lyon and Geneva for originating passengers**

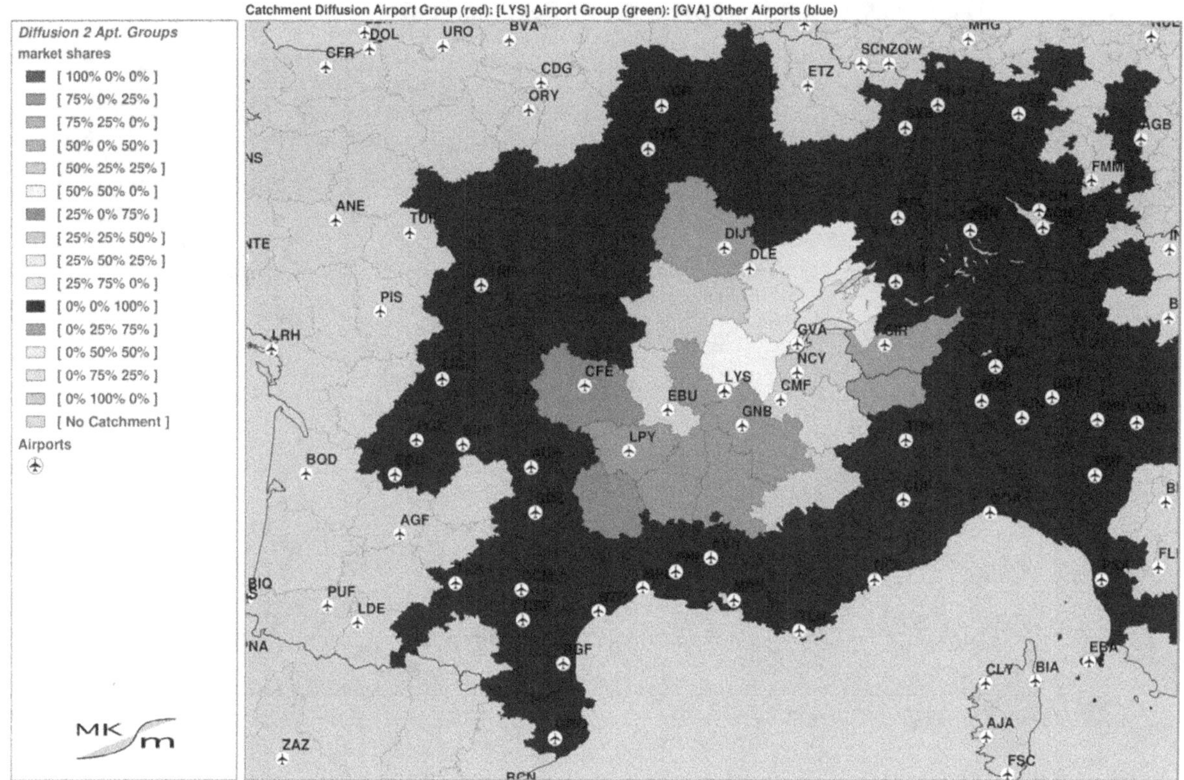

Long-term forecasts

It should be mentioned that modelling air transport as described in the previous chapters is not limited for status quo analyses or short term estimations on passenger potentials for new routes, but also can be used for long term forecasts, as executed for example in the early 1990s for the airport system of Berlin with a long term forecast for the year 2010.

Within this long-term forecast were considered:

- the political framework
- the planned development of surface transport infrastructure
- the network development according to demand for the Berlin airports as well as for their competitors.

Covering all those aspects led – from today's point of view – to a quite realistic estimation of the passenger demand until 2010, although it should be mentioned that at the time of forecasting (1993) the identified demand for Berlin of 23 million passengers in 2010, was criticised, as several other forecasts with standard models promoted much higher passenger volumes for Berlin, reaching in maximum up to 60 million passengers. These optimistic forecasts resulted out of enthusiastic assumptions blinded by the development of the first booming years after German reunification concerning the trends in passenger figures at the Berlin airports and economic development of the city, while neglecting any long term effects on modal split by new built or upgraded railway lines, the strategies of leading European network carriers, the development in air transport in neighbouring Poland and many other components of serious forecasting which were not considered adequately.

Figure 3.13. **Long term forecast Berlin (1993 to 2010)**

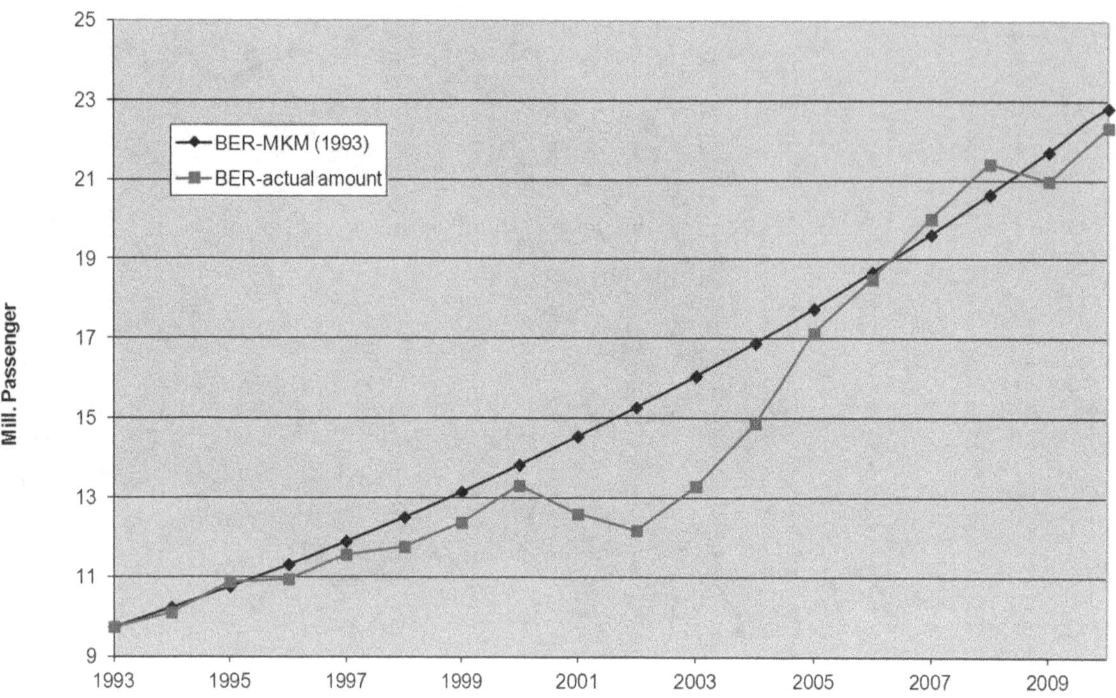

It has to be noted that the executed forecast just concerned a point forecast for the year 2010 and the values depicted in the figure are based on an interpolation from 1993 to 2010 for visualisation purposes.

Conclusions

Since the 1990's the market conditions for air transport have undergone multiple changes. Global drivers have been the liberalisation and deregulation policy as well as the globalisation of economy with new emerging markets. Stable markets have become unstable as economic drivers gain power and unpredictable incidents have direct effect on air transport. In parallel the competitive situation within the aviation world is facing an ongoing consolidation with bankruptcy and mergers as well as rising powerful airlines and airports and an east-ward displacement of the centre of economic gravity. New aircrafts change network strategies and new air service products emerged which are marketed differently using new electronic distribution channels. It is obvious that all these developments severely influenced the consumer behaviour.

To stay competitive and to develop air transport further all aviation stakeholders need to understand the consumer behaviour and the related elasticity to service characteristics in detail, but the available traditional data sources are declining rapidly so that the classic aviation forecasting tools become risky and are becoming less useful, as stated by IATA.

In this paper an alternative way for air transport demand forecasting is outlined reflecting the consumers' decision process. This approach considers the determinants of transport and airports, as well as air services, as a part of a competitive transport system linked with surface mode networks. Modelling the consumers' perspective requires considering their actual start and end points of journeys. In consequence mobility is a matter of regional attractiveness and the distribution is influenced by spatial divergence as regions compete for investments and tourists. The accessibility of the regions is determined by a choice set of travel options which concerns a portfolio of alternatives where originating and destination airports, as well as transfer possibilities, vary.

The decision taken by the consumers for the transport alternatives from the region of origin to the destination region is modelled in a consistent way of interdependent choice models which reflect the mode choice, airport and route choice, access/egress and slot choice. These models mirror the consumer behaviour using logistic functions whereby the mathematical form is flexible such that threshold and captivities can be captured. The elasticities of consumers to characteristics of the alternatives (e.g. time, cost, frequency, alliance) allow to measure demand effects on changes of the transport system, e.g. services, infrastructure.

This complex modelling approach allows considering local and global competition, and instead of fixed catchments the approach deals with dynamic ones determined by the attractiveness of the alternative transport opportunities available for each trip. Thus overlapping catchments and route competitors for short and long haul services can be analysed individually as the short- or long-term demand forecast for an airport or a route always considers the competitors endogenously as explained by some examples.

The price to run such a system approach is complexity in modelling, extensive computing power and intensive data collection (although the latter are mostly public data often available with a delay). One challenge is the aviation industry's sensitivity to market information, preventing access to sales data, consumer surveys, or even aircraft movement data. Another challenge is prevailing, large differences in publication rules for air transport statistics across Europe and throughout the world, making the data harmonisation process intensive and the validation process irreplaceable.

Notes

1. Billing Settlement Plan

2. Market Information Data Tapes

3 See http://www.oag.com/schedules

4. http://www.worldtek.com/wp-content/uploads/2011/10/Direct-Data-Services-Wilson.pdf

5. http://www.directdataservice.com/

6. http://www.sita.aero/surveys-reports/industry-surveys-reports/airline-it-trends-survey-2013

7. http://corporate.airfrance.com/en/press/news/article/item/3-questions-for-lionel-guerin-chairman-and-ceo-of-hop/

8. Indication for commercial data source

9. Having access to the 10% ticket sample in the US as non-US citizen and combining this with a 10% ticket sample for Europe, which is technically possible with minor effort and costs for airlines, would open a new dimension for researchers and modelling.

10. EUROCONTROL refuses sharing schedule-related data with the argument that the information belongs to the airlines, which is disconcerting as airlines publish schedules but unfortunately not consistently in one place consistently.

11. What effects appear in case a certain activity would have taken place in the reference year.

12. http://epp.eurostat.ec.europa.eu/portal/page/portal/nuts_nomenclature/introduction

13. http://www.hacon.de/hafas-en

References

Gaudry M., Heinitz F., Last J., Mandel B., (1998), "Methodological Developments within the Quasi-Direct Format Demand Structure: the Multicountry Application for Passengers MAP-1", Strategic European Multi-Modal Modelling, *Working Paper BETA n°9815*.

Gaudry M., Mandel B., Rothengatter W., (1994a) "Entwicklung eines gekoppelten Verkehrs Erzeugungs- und verteilungsmodells für den Personenfernverkehr" – "Development of a linked trip generation and distribution model for long distance passenger traffic", on behalf of the German Ministry of Transport FENr.: 60307/92; Université de Montréal C.R.T., MKmetric GmbH - University of Karlsruhe (TH) Institute of Economic Policy and Research (IWW).

Gaudry M., Mandel B., Rothengatter W., (1994b) "Introducing Spatial Competition through an Autoregressive Contiguous Distributed (AR-C-D) Process in Intercity Generation-Distribution Models within a Quasi-Direct Format (QDF)", Université de Montréal C.R.T., CRT-971, MKmetric GmbH - Karlsruhe, University of Karlsruhe (TH) Institute of Economic Policy and Research (IWW).

Mandel B., (1999a), "Airport Choice & Competition - a Strategic Approach", 3rd Air Transport Research Group (ATRG) Conference, Hong Kong.

Mandel B., (1999b), "The Interdependency of Airport Choice and Travel Demand" in Gaudry, M. and R. Mayes *Taking stock of air liberalization*, Proceedings of the International Symposium at the ICAO; 189-222, Kluwer Academic Press.

Mandel B., (1999c), *Measuring Competition in Air Transport; Airports and Air Traffic - Regulation, Privatisation and Competition*, Peter Lang Press.

Mandel B., Gaudry M., Rothengatter W., (1994) "Linear or Non-linear Utility Functions in Logit Models? The Impact on German High Speed Rail Demand Forecasts", *Transportation Research Journal Vol. 28B*, Elsevier Science Ltd.

Mandel B., (1992), "Schnellverkehr und Modal Split" – "High Speed Transport and Modal Split", Baden Baden: Nomos Verlag.

ORGANISATION FOR ECONOMIC CO-OPERATION AND DEVELOPMENT

The OECD is a unique forum where governments work together to address the economic, social and environmental challenges of globalisation. The OECD is also at the forefront of efforts to understand and to help governments respond to new developments and concerns, such as corporate governance, the information economy and the challenges of an ageing population. The Organisation provides a setting where governments can compare policy experiences, seek answers to common problems, identify good practice and work to co-ordinate domestic and international policies.

The OECD member countries are: Australia, Austria, Belgium, Canada, Chile, the Czech Republic, Denmark, Estonia, Finland, France, Germany, Greece, Hungary, Iceland, Ireland, Israel, Italy, Japan, Korea, Luxembourg, Mexico, the Netherlands, New Zealand, Norway, Poland, Portugal, the Slovak Republic, Slovenia, Spain, Sweden, Switzerland, Turkey, the United Kingdom and the United States. The European Union takes part in the work of the OECD.

OECD Publishing disseminates widely the results of the Organisation's statistics gathering and research on economic, social and environmental issues, as well as the conventions, guidelines and standards agreed by its members.

OECD PUBLISHING, 2, rue André-Pascal, 75775 PARIS CEDEX 16
(74 2016 02 1 P) ISBN 978-92-82-10801-7 – 2016

www.ingramcontent.com/pod-product-compliance
Lightning Source LLC
LaVergne TN
LVHW061251100826
845148LV00008B/1098